WOMEN ALONE

Some Interesting Food for Thought:

According to the 1994 *Information Please Almanac,* in the
United States, there are:
- 127,470,455 females;
- 11,692,000 families maintained by women only;
- 11,477,000 widows;
- 1,165,400 births to unmarried women each year;
- approximately 2,362,000 marriages each year; and
- approximately 1,215,000 divorces each year.

The life expectancy for a female at birth is 79 years;
for a male, it is 72 years.

WOMEN ALONE

Creating a Joyous and Fulfilling Life

Julie Keene
and
Ione Jenson

Hay House, Inc.
Carson, CA

Copyright © 1995 by Julie Keene and Ione Jenson

Published and distributed in the United States by:

Hay House, Inc.
1154 E. Dominguez St.
P.O. Box 6204
Carson, CA 90749-6204
(800) 654-5126

Edited by: Jill Kramer
Designed by: Atlis Graphics & Design, Mechanicsburg, PA 17055

"Newspaper Ad": Permission granted by Ann Landers and
 Creators Syndicate
Excerpts from "Loners on Wheels" and Erin O'Regan's story:
Permission granted by *The Spokesman Review,* Spokane, WA
"Circle" poem: Permission granted by Gordon Yaswen

Library of Congress Cataloging-in-Publication Data

Keene, Julie.
    Women alone: creating a joyous and fulfilling life / Julie Keene
    and Ione Jenson.
        p.   cm.
    Includes bibliographical references.
    ISBN 1-56170-119-X
    1. Single women—United States. I. Jenson, Ione.II. Title

ISBN 1-56170-119-X

99 98 97 96 95   5 4 3 2 1

First Printing, April 1995

Printed in the United States of America

❖ ❖ ❖

We dedicate this book to all the women who have been willing to be modern pioneers and create rich and meaningful lives for themselves regardless of outer circumstances, and who have then so willingly and lovingly shared their stories.

❖ ❖ ❖

C O N T E N T S

THE DESIRE TO PARTNER

*"Never doubt that a small group of thoughtful, committed citizens
can change the world: Indeed it's the only thing that ever has."*

— Margaret Mead

There seems to be an innate desire among a majority of women to both partner and to co-parent. We, Julie and Ione, made that choice ourselves during an earlier period of our lives, and we honor and applaud that decision. However, we have also noted that the most successful partnerships are generally those where two whole and complete individuals merge. Women who have solid ego boundaries and a strong sense of their own psychological and spiritual identities are usually significantly more successful in attaining happy and lasting relationships of all kinds.

Within each one of us is an indomitable, conquering spirit, and it is that spirit that made America great. It pioneered the West; it survived wars and the Great Depression. People banded together and found ways to cope when times seemed impossible. They turned their homes into beauty parlors, barber shops, grocery stores, neighborhood laundries, and lived in basements or small rear quarters. They found creative ways to survive, and small ways to enjoy life. They pooled meals, played games, and helped and encouraged one another. They grew gardens together during the second world war and shared produce. Times may have been tough, but these hardy souls rose to the challenge.

As women alone, we, too, can rise to the challenge. We can band together and find extraordinary resources within ourselves and one another. We cannot only survive, but we can create a joyous and fulfilling life as well. However, to do so, we may need to move from the solely nuclear blood family paradigm that has long existed into a new way of thinking that encompasses different kinds of nonrelated-family experiences and support systems.

In order to continue to exist and evolve, throughout history human beings have been driven to face their problems squarely and then move on to seek and find solutions. Certainly, we have not become so naive and soft in the past few relatively prosperous decades that we expect the government or someone else to come and solve our problems magically! We must face the changing cultural norms, as well as the challenges involved in being women alone. We must honestly evaluate what we need and want to have happen, and then go to work to change our lives in new and constructive ways.

Most of us are born alone, and we die alone. So, since aloneness seems to be one of the major lessons of Earth School, and since most women will spend some portion of their lives alone, we need to confront the issue in a powerful and constructive manner. If each of us will take responsibility for our own happiness and not try to project that responsibility onto someone else, we will have formed a reliable and healthy partnership within ourselves. Once that has been attained, we are more likely to sustain solid relationships with others. As we go about living rich, full, and meaningful lives, we are bound to meet many people who are on a similar journey. Inevitably, that will put us in touch with individuals whom we might relate to on deeper levels.

The real issue here is not to put life on "hold" until that happens. Don't keep your good dishes and nice linens in a closet until you marry or partner. Provide and make a beautiful home for yourself. Then, if one day you and another choose to share the great adventure of life in an intimate living experience, you will enter into it from a rich inner space—not out of desperate need or longing.

Making partnership with another the major or sole focus of our existence or reason for being is an unhealthy and co-dependent lifestyle, and it seldom works well. Marriages and other close relationships take time and effort, and the participants must be loving and supportive of each other's psychospiritual journey if the union is to succeed. Whether we find someone with whom to partner, or whether we even choose to partner, we still need to be creative in exploring life and unfolding our own inner agenda for personal growth.

Every woman needs to be able to relate to other people, and she also needs to be able to relate to herself. Why not learn to create a life that will be able to give you a healthy balance of both without allowing your happiness to depend solely on outer circumstances! You are the only human being you can always really count on, so learn to live and be happy and productive either way.

The time has come to stop feeling helpless, to stop playing the role of the victim, and to once again become a creator of a new paradigm that includes women alone who are living productive, joyous, and fulfilling lives while being supported by other loving and caring human beings—that is, being "all one" instead of just feeling "a lone"!

— Julie Keene and Ione Jenson
   Hayden, Idaho

ACKNOWLEDGMENTS

Our sincere thanks to the staff at Hay House for their encouragement and efforts to help us launch this book. We would especially like to thank our editor, Jill Kramer, for her patience with all our questions and for all the suggestions that helped us to expand and enhance the quality of this work. We also want to express our gratitude to Alan and Chuck Jenson for their patience in providing computer support and expertise. We truly appreciate the enthusiasm and support of our friends all around the country who are too numerous to name individually. We love and appreciate you all!

FLYING SOLO

"If I have to, I can do anything. I am strong,
I am invincible, I am woman."

— Helen Reddy

An increasing number of men and women are finding themselves alone; for some it will be temporary, for others a permanent state. According to the 1990 U.S. Census figures, the percentage of single adults in this country reached nearly 40 percent of the total population. Twenty years earlier, the single population comprised only 26 percent. Perhaps even more significant is the fact that women today make up almost two-thirds of the single populace. Many women will be alone for a lifetime, while others will be alone for only sporadic periods. Nevertheless, even those women who are interested in eventually forming a partnership with a man need not hold back from making the most of life and enjoying it, whatever their present circumstances. Unfortunately, our society often places challenging obstacles in the path of the woman alone.

Although attitudes about single women are slowly changing, we certainly have a long way to go. Women who never marry are still sometimes perceived as "old maids"; divorcees or widows are often looked upon with pity or suspicion; and single women (especially senior citizens) are still viewed by some as easy targets for financial scams. Consequently, a great many women who find themselves alone don't want to be in this state any longer than absolutely necessary.

Evidence of the desperate desire of millions of women to escape aloneness can be found in the personal ad section of most newspapers and magazines, where a multitude of women seek male companionship. (Yes, we know that men place those ads, too, but since this book is about women, we will just focus on that segment of society here.) Yet, we know those ads reflect only the tip of the iceberg. Even more women would like to find companionship but do not resort to overt advertising.

On the other hand, there are many women who appreciate the single lifestyle and consciously choose it (we have interviewed some of these women and will discuss this choice in Chapter One). These women no longer cling to the age-old concept that marriage is the only path to a happy life; they have found rich and meaningful alternatives.

For many years we have been presenting personal growth workshops across the country. Wherever we go, we meet women caught up in the trials of being alone, as well as women who are living out creative alternatives to the challenges of being single. We are delighted to see so many innovative solutions being applied, and in this book, we look at what several women, including ourselves, have done to meet the demands of being alone and how we have discovered some very satisfying options.

We focus initially on some of the fears that arise when a woman comes to the realization that she is alone and may well spend the rest of her life in that state. One of the most immediate challenges she faces is the numbing feeling of loneliness, that almost nightmarish realization that no one is close enough to touch her or to care about her day-to-day existence. Many women report that the hours alone after work and on weekends and holidays often become times of overwhelming despair. Even when children or other family members live close by, their lives are usually so full that women alone sometimes find that only a very limited portion of their loneliness is alleviated by the attention of relatives. Not only that, but many women have family members who live a great distance from their homes, and, of course, there are women we interviewed who have no living relatives.

However, we must acknowledge that loneliness is not strictly confined to those who find themselves living alone. We spoke with a retired physician who is married and, therefore, doesn't qualify as a "woman alone," but she reminded us: "You don't have to be single to be alone. Indifference is the worst kind of aloneness there is." We agree that we must all ultimately face our aloneness no matter what our living arrangement.

Julie spent many years wrestling with feelings of loneliness and inadequacy while searching for the "right and perfect" man in spite of the fact that she became involved in the women's movement and taught a college-level women's studies class. She believed from a very early age that true happiness could only be found with a "Prince Charming" who would help her live "happily ever after." Although she has always had women friends, her children, her work, and other interests, there have been times in her life when she felt desperately lonely. After her children left home, she remembers often coming home from teaching at the end of the day to an empty house. Much of the time this was no problem. Other times a feeling of isolation and desolation would overtake her, and she'd think, If the floor opened up and I disappeared from the face of the earth, who would know or care? At those times, she felt that she could not call friends and impose her depression upon them; she simply suffered through it by herself.

Closely related to the feelings of loneliness that many women experience is the "I'm nothing without a man" attitude. Instead of seeking productive solutions to loneliness, too many women put their lives on hold, waiting for that "right and perfect" man to come along and fix it. Too often, they become addicted to the idea of romance and, thus, get caught up in inappropriate relationships. Julie feels that she spent too many years of her life doing just that. She is not alone. Many women commented that they felt something was missing in their lives and that they were only half a person if they were single. Some of these same women expressed the fear that something must be wrong with them or they would not be without a man. As such, too many women stay in destructive relationships because they feel that even an abusive relationship or one with a married man is better than no relationship at all. Ann Landers once featured a newspaper ad in her column that had been answered by a number of women:

WANTED: Girlfriend. Single or married. Good-looking, sexy, intelligent companion between 30 and 40. Must be extremely flexible and undemanding. Willing to tryst approximately one night a week (for at least two hours, preferably at your house). Prefer to stay in and have dinner cooked (will provide occasional bottle of wine) since going out in public presents risks. Possibility of one or two overnight weekends a year, if convenient for me and you are available, discreet, and willing to pay your own way. Must be a good listener, have a strong sex drive, and be aggressive, but not pushy. Willing to wait for convenient time to hear from me about time and place to get together. Must not try to contact me by phone. Too risky. Possibility for long-term relationship if you can wait it out until my kids are out of high school—unless I meet someone who is less demanding or more accessible.

— MARRIED BUT NEEDING MORE

While it may seem absurd, that ad elicited dozens of responses from women willing to do anything to have a man in their lives!

Another fear expressed again and again is that of living alone. Different from loneliness, it encompasses many other aspects of being alone that are physical as well as emotional. There is the fear of being ill and unable to care for oneself or even unable to call for help when it might be desperately needed. One woman told us: "I had to have my wisdom teeth pulled, and although I asked several people, there was no one available to take me or bring me home from the dentist. The fact that no one cared enough to arrange their schedule to help me with this simple request reinforced my fears of living alone."

Another woman exploring her fear of living alone posed this question: "Who will attend to things when I can't?" She had needed foot surgery, and in those first few days following the operation when it was necessary to stay totally off her feet, there wasn't anyone to help her with meals, take care of a few necessary errands, or to "even bring me a glass of water"! Loneliness was not the issue— she is a busy professional woman who enjoys her time alone reading, writing, and just generally relaxing, but certain physical realities made her see that living alone had huge disadvantages. She confided that her current fear is: "How will I manage if some big catastrophe happens?" Worrying about illness or physical disability seems to be an almost universal issue for the woman who is alone.

Other women say that they are afraid to live alone because they fear physical violence. They believe that women are usually safer if someone else is around, and they are concerned about the increasing reports of men who prey on single women. Some women find that when the sun goes down, they become filled with apprehension and are aware of every little sound. They also dislike entering the house alone after dark and find that they often hesitate to go out in the evening for that very reason.

Another troubling issue common to women alone relates to finances. Many women find living alone a financial burden and are often forced to live on incomes near or below the national poverty level. One in every six women in the U.S. is a displaced homemaker—divorced, widowed, or separated. The poverty rate among single mothers is an incredible 44 percent, while at the same time, the poverty rate for ALL households is only 11 percent. (These statistics are based on 1990 Census Bureau data and reported by the advocacy group Women Work!, which tracks economic trends.)

Consequently, that oft-heard fear of becoming a "bag lady" is not all that farfetched. Even Gloria Steinem, a powerful force in the women's movement, confessed in a television interview that she has this fear from time to time. But in true Steinem fashion, she said that she comforts herself with the thought that if she should ever become a bag lady, "I'll organize them!" Not a bad alternative, and certainly a creative way of facing her fear. However, unlike Gloria, a vast number of women alone do not have the education or skills to support themselves in comfort. The fear of being homeless becomes more than just a fear; it is an ever-present possibility.

Many single older women are concerned about who will make health decisions for them if they are not capable of making choices for themselves. They fear that uncaring family members will take steps that are convenient for themselves, rather than choices that are in line with what the single woman herself might have chosen. Older women also have qualms about the loss of independence that would result from not being able to drive or get their license renewed. One woman who lost her eyesight attested, "It's my worst nightmare come true!"

There are probably as many other fears and concerns as there are single women, but these are the most fundamental concerns that have been expressed, time and time again, as we talked with women who are alone, and it doesn't seem to matter whether these women have been alone for their entire adult lives or whether they have just recently entered into the solitary state. However, in spite of many seemingly overwhelming fears, we have confidence that creative solutions can be found for women alone.

We now look at how several women, including ourselves, have faced the challenges of being alone. We focus upon some creative alternatives and look at the steps that women can take to overcome their fears and thus live and express freely as self-actualized and productive human beings. It is our wish that every woman who reads this book will reach out and create even more unique options for herself.

❖ ❖ ❖

CONQUERING LONELINESS

"I must conquer my loneliness alone;
I must be happy with myself or
I have nothing to offer you."

— Peter McWilliams, author

Women alone need to be creative in their search for alternative routes to a full and happy life. So often all energies, thoughts, and hopes are directed toward finding the perfect man, and while there is certainly nothing wrong with male companionship or with a happy marriage, there is something amiss if we cannot be equally happy alone. As women get older, statistics reveal that the chances of getting married decrease dramatically. Growing numbers of single women are not involved with a male on a mutually committed basis. When a woman develops only a sexual liaison with a male, he is often married and unavailable for much except the bedroom experience, and nothing of lasting value is likely to come from the encounter. Only rarely is such a superficial relationship all that a woman wants; it is unlikely that her emotional needs will be satisfied in this way. Most women desire more permanence in their lives, and yet to postpone full and rich enjoyment of life until "Mr. Right" happens by is a mistake that literally wastes precious years of living.

Fortunately, there is a way out of this dilemma. Women alone can go beyond the accustomed social attitudes and find meaning and richness through a variety of quite feasible choices that are available to us! Our cultural norm has created an illusion that the state of marriage is perfect and that the states of widowhood, divorce, and single life are far less desirable and on a lower level than that of matrimony. We do not, however, have to continue to subscribe to this dehumanizing myth, for there are no absolutes. Relationships of all kinds, including those with friends and family, are characterized by difficult times, even as they offer grand opportunities for personal learning and growth. Therefore, if a woman alone resolves to live a happy, full life while keeping the option of the "right man" as only one alternative in a long list of fruitful possibilities, she begins to put everything into its proper perspective!

By dissolving the cultural illusion that having the right man is the only true way to ultimate happiness, a woman frees herself to look at the various ways that other women alone meet their needs and create a life of depth and meaning for themselves. Being addicted to finding a partner is as unhealthy as remaining in an abusive or dysfunctional relationship, as harmful as any other addiction. One single woman whom we interviewed stated, "I'm open to the possibility of marriage, but if it never happens, I'll be just fine." When more women alone can say that and truly mean it, a significant amount of progress will have been made.

The World Is for People, Not Just for Couples

We are always amazed by the myriad ways in which bold and self-reliant women have created a satisfying lifestyle for themselves. Most of these women have learned to set strong ego boundaries. They have concluded that their happiness does not lie outside themselves, but that it is truly an internal attitude and an act of will. They have come to the realization that they alone must ultimately take the responsibility for their own well-being.

We met such a woman a few years ago in a campground at Pacifica, California. She was 57 at the time, and her husband had died three years earlier. After working through her initial grief, she decided to sell her house and buy a motorhome. It was an immense vehicle, and she carried a bicycle on the front and towed a small car behind. She was on her way home after spending seven months in Mexico, where she had taken Spanish and had become very involved in the local culture. Although she wasn't really ready to leave Mexico, a business at home needed attention. She decided to go back and sell the business because there was still so much she wanted to do—such as spending extended amounts of time in Alaska and Eastern Canada. She figured she could sell the business, invest the money, and use the interest to roam. She was having a wonderful time. It had never been difficult for her to find someone who wanted an inexpensive vacation to go along with her for a few weeks when she felt the desire for company. The only cost to her companion was food and airfare home after the trip. She enjoyed traveling to a particular area, living there for several months, and getting involved in the local scenery. She knew she wouldn't engage in this lifestyle forever, but was determined to do so for as long as she felt rewarded by the experience.

This woman could have been lost in her grief and loneliness after a long and happy marriage, but she chose to live life differently. She did not deny her grief processes; she did not repress her feelings, but after a time, she realized that it was up to her to deal with the situation that life had presented to her and to find a new way of living. She was truly giving it all she had.

Now, it's certainly not necessary for us to uproot our homes and move to a new country or state in order to live life more fully as women alone. There are many things we can do while remaining in the comfortable world that we have always lived in. For example:

Pen Pals / Computer Networking/Correspondence

Some women find letter writing a rich source of intimacy. Letters may be sent to pen pals whose names have been garnered from many different sources. These pen pals may reside in distant or foreign geographical locations and impart interesting details about cultural differences. One can do extensive armchair traveling in this manner. The best source is your local library; ask your librarian to help you find resources for writing to pen pals in different countries. Or, you may contact: WORLDWIDE PEN FRIENDS, P.O. Box 6896, Thousand Oaks, CA 91359-6896.

In addition, computer owners who have modems have the opportunity to expand their horizons. They can subscribe to bulletin boards and networks of various kinds, depending on the area of interest. Many people meet and communicate with each other in this manner and find much companionship and enjoyment, as well as a wealth of knowledge and self-improvement. Computer magazines feature ads for the various on-line networks, and your nearest computer store can give you additional information if you need it.

There are also those women who correspond frequently with shut-ins and who find themselves learning what it feels like to live an extremely limited physical existence. One of these women said that she and her correspondent were "tape-pals" and sent cassette tapes back and forth at the rate of two or three a month. For them, tapes were quicker and easier and allowed them to communicate more often. They use a 30-minute tape, and each has her name on one side. In this way, they can re-listen to what they've said and then turn the tape over and listen to their pal's response. The respondent then tapes over her own previous message. They've been doing this for several years now and have become very close friends.

Others keep a steady stream of correspondence going with the various friends they've made throughout the years, or with widely scattered family members. Round-robin letters sometime go on for decades among family members or close friends.

Several women have noted that they find it easier to express themselves in an open and intimate manner through letters as opposed to in-person communication. Pen pals share details about their families and all the traumas of daily living. They may share their feelings, their hopes, and dreams. Each person can share without interruption and feel as though they have had an opportunity to thoroughly express themselves, something that doesn't often happen in everyday conversation, where give-and-take is the norm. Corresponding regularly with an assortment of pen pals can be a very real and meaningful way to feel connected and intimate with other human beings.

The Rewards of Journaling

Another form that writing may take is journaling, which we have found to be a valuable and insightful experience. Journaling is an excellent way to express intimate thoughts and feelings when one is alone. Different from keeping a diary, which is merely a record of events, a journal allows us to give expression to our deepest musings and allows us to record our responses to the events that are occurring in our lives.

Women who live alone all too often keep their deepest emotions locked inside them, a state of affairs that can often manifest as physical and mental problems. Research is providing more and more scientific evidence that links stress to illness in our minds and bodies, and it's been found that people who write about traumatic events that they've never shared with anyone before actually boost their immune system for up to six weeks!

Early pioneer women, who suffered from extreme isolation and loneliness much of the time, found a great deal of consolation through the journaling process. This was an outlet for reflecting upon their lives and for recording tales about the adventure and rigors of life on the frontier. We now are able to read published copies of some of these journals. They enable us know the authors and their inner processes, and they give us an opportunity to share in the often bittersweet adventures of our sisters during the earlier days of America's history. It is difficult to overestimate the value of journaling!

Hobbies for Those Empty Hours

Many women tell us that hobbies enrich their lives and fill in those empty hours that would otherwise be spent alone. They take classes to learn all types of different skills, or join clubs with like-minded people, spending many happy hours of companionship with fellow hobbyists. They sometimes earn money working at the hobby of their choice, taking items to craft fairs, flea markets, consignment shops, selling items to specialty stores, or advertising and marketing on their own.

Many women are delving into writing classes, autobiography classes, photography, painting, pottery, and crafts of all kinds. They are participating in sports, enjoying antique collecting, and traveling. There are hobbies that fit into almost anyone's budget, ranging from items made from scraps and discards to things that are quite costly. Perusing catalogs, stores, newspapers, and magazines should be enough to give anyone a number of ideas.

The Joy of Pets

Many women who live alone find that taking care of pets of all kinds, such as dogs, cats, birds, or even more exotic animals, is a wonderful way to alleviate loneliness. Pets need lots of attention, and they take us outside of ourselves and give us a reason to think about the welfare of another living being. Pets respond to love and give generous quantities of affection in return. For many people alone, another live body in the house to touch and to hold gives a remarkable texture and dimension to life.

There are many ways to obtain the perfect pet. Ads appear in local newspapers and in various specialized magazines, there are dog and cat shows, animal shelters (a wonderful place to find a pet that desperately needs a home), and often neighbors and friends who have pets to give away. Of course, there are pet stores, but some of the animals from these establishments are overbred or simply not healthy. The most important thing to remember is: Pets can really change people's lives!

Volunteering Helps!

Whether you have a full-time job or not, you can usually find the time to set aside a few hours here and there to lend a helping hand to worthwhile organizations in your community. Your service will be greatly appreciated, and you'll reap many personal benefits if you choose a project that truly interests you. If you peruse your local newspaper and keep your ears open, you will find that there will be plenty of opportunities to use your skills and allow creative expression.

For example, hospitals always need extra help and often have an auxiliary that organizes volunteers. They need people to do everything from holding babies, wheeling patients to their rooms, and delivering flowers, to doing clerical work.

Many schools love having community involvement. They appreciate help with assisting teachers, or in sharing some skill or area of expertise as a guest lecturer or mentor. If one school isn't open to outside help, don't give up—seek out another. You're sure to find one that will welcome you with open arms.

When Julie lived in Tallahassee, Florida, the local newspaper carried a column once a week called "The Caring Connection." This column profiled four different people in the community with special needs, and it listed the name of a social service agency person to contact if you could help. It also reported on the responses from the previous week, and it was heartwarming to see how many people's needs were being met in this manner.

If you're an adventurous person and have the freedom to take off for weeks or months to volunteer for charitable causes, you can investigate that possibility by reading the new edition of *Invest Yourself: The Catalogue of Volunteer Opportunities.* This book lists more than 200 organizations that are in need of volunteer help, many of them abroad. It's indexed in several ways, both by location and by categories of skills and interests. It covers 45 countries and most states in the U.S., with listings for volunteers younger than 18, as well as for adults. It also features testimonials of volunteers who point out the benefits gained from volunteering. (The book can be ordered for $9.95 from The Commission on Voluntary Service and Action, P.O. Box 117, New York, NY 10009.) In addition, the Peace Corps and Vista both provide excellent opportunities for service, adventure, and change.

Rewarding volunteer options are also available for those over 60. Elderhostel, which offers vital and vigorous older adults a safe and satisfying route to public service, now puts out a special edition devoted entirely to service programs both in the U.S. and abroad. Whether older volunteers help build affordable houses in poor American communities, teach English in eastern Europe, or count endangered sea mammals in the Caribbean, they extend their personal limits in serving others while living and working with a team of 10 to 20 people. (For more information, write Elderhostel at Box 1751, Wakefield, MA 01880.)

We do free-lance work, but we also like to donate some portion of our time and talent to a worthwhile project. Since we are counselors, workshop leaders, and writers on spiritual and personal growth issues, we volunteer these skills from time to time when our schedule permits. For example, we will do an occasional free counseling session for someone who is willing to help him/herself, but who needs a little boost, and we donate counseling time to our local women's center. Because Ione is also a former educator, she was able to help an alternative elementary school go through its growing pains when it was formed. She has occasionally offered to do a free workshop for a local preschool and its parents and teachers, and she spent six weeks doing a once-a-week workshop on dreams for a group of enthusiastic high school students. Julie has also given time on a weekly basis to hospice workers and volunteers, helping them maintain their balance and perspective in the midst of the emotionally draining, yet critically important work they perform. She has been a Big Sister and has spent many satisfying hours with a Little Sister who needed extra attention. Those who volunteer reap many benefits, not the least of which is a true sense of community. Giving feels great!

The Surrogate Family

Several years ago, Ione lived in a university town where many people were thousands of miles away from their grandparents, aunts, uncles, and cousins. Ione's co-worker did something that seemed daring at the time, but she was a young woman of the sixties, and a lot of unconventional things were going on in the world. She placed an ad in the local newspaper, advertising for substitute grandparents for her two little ones. The ad read something like this: "WANTED: Our grandma and grandpa live far away, and we would like to find someone whose grandchildren are far away, too. We would like to have you come visit us, and maybe you could read us a book or help us bake cookies. If this sounds fun to you, too, please call us." The phone number and children's names and ages were listed. There were a surprising number of responses to that ad, and some warm long-term relationships were formed. Today, it would be a wonderful idea for a giving woman to place a similar ad, offering to be aunt, grandmother, or big sister to some children who could use some extra love and attention.

Personal Growth Groups

There is an abundance of personal growth and support groups these days. These groups are invaluable for people wanting to delve into their own inner processes and who want to make conscious changes in their lives and attitudes. The daily newspapers, and even our own mailboxes, offer us a wealth of information regarding times, dates, locations, and subject matter. Joining some groups can be quite costly, but there are also some that are very reasonable, or even free! The more costly seminars are usually associated with "big-name people," but equally valuable information can be elicited at a much lower price from people who have just as much expertise, but who don't happen to be nationally known. You can always find something of interest that will fit your budget! Just keep your eyes and ears open.

Local YWCAs usually offer women's programs and support groups on an ongoing basis, so if there is one of these organizations in your area, call and ask to be on their mailing list. Senior citizen centers in many localities offer a variety of groups, classes, and activities; and local newspapers nearly always have a section listing community events. Here you will find seminars, support groups, art shows, craft fairs, sporting events, and various other activities that are taking place in your area. Sometimes it can be difficult to take that first step to go out and get acquainted with new people, but extending ourselves is essential if we want to avoid being alone and lonely.

Do/Learn Something New

Another way to get out there and be more a part of life is to return to school, take workshops being offered, or audit some classes at a nearby college. Try writing a book. Even if you never get it published, the experience will tap the depths of your being and encourage you to express yourself in new and creative ways. If being an author doesn't appeal to you, learn to dance, or try painting a picture. Even a box of the watercolor paints we used in elementary school can set your inner child free to express, both in color and form, some aspects of yourself...no matter how primitive! If you haven't already entered the computer generation, learn to use a word processor or computer. We looked at our computer with apprehension, thinking that we could NEVER learn how to work this electronic wonder, but a son in the computer science field convinced us that we could, and we did! Needless to say, we love our computer, and this book is both evidence of our willingness to learn how to use it, and our ability to express ourselves as authors. We all have something valuable to say; try it if you have a mind to do so.

Travel

Although many times it's possible to find a friend to travel with, this is not always the case. Please don't give up on the idea of taking a trip just because you have to travel alone! Several years ago, Julie decided that she wanted to travel to Hawaii for spring break. No friend or fellow faculty member was available to go with her, so she decided to go alone, albeit with some fears. She booked a tour with a local travel agent and went on an excursion with a group of 20 strangers. As it turned out, the people on the tour were quite friendly, and there were other single women about her age who were traveling by themselves as well. With the additional side-trips that were part of the tour, she was as involved as she wanted to be. Her experience helped her realize that it's possible for a woman to enjoy herself and feel confident and secure on a trip that she takes by herself.

A few years ago, we traveled, along with two other single women friends, to Greece, Egypt, and Israel. Before joining this church tour group of 20, we only knew the minister, but we soon became acquainted with the others. This group also included several single women traveling alone who readily became friendly with each other, as well as with the other members of the group. Being alone didn't prevent anybody from thoroughly enjoying themselves!

If you're the type of person who likes to travel with a purpose, as opposed to just seeing the sights, we recommend some of the educational tours that are available. As we mentioned previously, if you're over 60, Elderhostel is an excellent way to travel, learn, and meet new people. A few years ago we purchased a 21-foot motorhome and set out to see the United States. We financed our adventure by presenting personal growth workshops in churches. One of the workshops dealt with the challenges involved in being a woman alone. Because Ione is a psychologist, and Julie is an ordained minister, we had the credentials and contacts to make our venture a reality, and we were very grateful for the opportunity. We found an abundance of RV parks everywhere we traveled, and when feasible, simply parked our motorhome in the churchyard where we were presenting a workshop. We covered the entire country, from New England to Florida, the Midwest, the South, and the West Coast. We even made our way to Bermuda and Hawaii by offering workshops in those tropical paradises.

While driving around the country in our motorhome, we occasionally encountered people who were surprised that two women alone would be traveling about in this manner, but we never once felt that we weren't up to the challenges inherent in our adventure!

Of course, if you don't have anyone to travel with and you'd like to take to the open road, you can certainly do it by yourself. We met two mature women ministers who often travel alone. One has a van with a Merry Miler sleeper on top; the other has her own small motorhome. Neither uses her single state as an excuse to avoid traveling wherever she wants to go, and they each travel the country at will whenever they please.

There is even a club for people who travel alone in their RVs. Columnist Cathy Free, writing for the *Spokesman-Review* in Spokane, Washington, captured the fun and adventure of it all. The following is an excerpt from her column:

> Creston, B.C.— "Big Mama" is 25 feet long, purrs like a Ferrari, and has been known to stop traffic—especially on winding canyon roads. "Isn't she sexy?" says 71-year-old Retta Semz, stepping inside the unique motor home, which is adorned in various shades of head-turning pink.
>
> Single since her divorce 30 years ago, Semz says she'll always be a loner. But she'll never be lonely. Not

with Loners on Wheels—a group of single RV enthusi-asts—to keep her company.

Tuesday morning, Semz slid behind Big Mama's wheel and headed across the Canadian border for a camp-out near Creston with other Inland Northwest Loners. Known as the WEIN-LOWS (Washington Eastern, Idaho North), the group's 16 members prefer campfire suppers and swatting mosquitoes to hassling with blind dates on the singles scene.

Founded 23 years ago by a Missouri woman who didn't want to go camping alone, Loners on Wheels has chapters in every state, from the Longhorn LOWS in Texas to the Pueb-LOWS in Arizona.

Unlike most singles clubs, making moon eyes over burnt marshmallows isn't tolerated by Loners. Members who want to zip their sleeping bags together are asked to go elsewhere. "If a couple meets at a camp-out and gets married, that's great," says WEIN-LOW president Dorothy Booth, "but then, you're out. You can't be a married Loner."

Booth, a retired teacher from Post Falls, Idaho, has pulled her 16-foot trailer across the country to mingle with other single campers. When her husband, John, died in 1968, she missed the traditional outings to Priest Lake. Booth longed for the aroma of a summer night in the woods, and tall tales around a crackling campfire. "I wanted somebody to camp with, but I didn't want to remarry," she says. "I found the answer in Loners on Wheels."

(Courtesy *Spokesman-Review,* Spokane, WA) (Loners On Wheels National Headquarters: P.O. Box 1355 Poplar Bluff, MO 63901)

Friendship with Ourselves and Others

Keeping some old friends and staying open to making new ones is essential to the happiness of a woman alone. However, it is also crucial that a woman become a friend to herself and spend happy and productive time alone. This is a challenge in our culture, which fosters the notion that if we're alone, there must be something wrong with us. It can take practice and perseverance to finally feel comfortable eating in a restaurant alone or going to a movie or concert by oneself, but we deprive ourselves of a great deal of pleasure if we simply stay home watching TV every day or night. Friends are not always near and available, so why make ourselves prisoners?

Making a date with yourself to go out alone on a particular day or evening is an excellent goal. Find an activity that interests you. It might be a film or a play you've been wanting to see, a restaurant you'd like to try, or a museum to amble through. Treat this "date" as a definite appointment that can't be broken any more than you would unnecessarily break a date with a beloved friend. What's most important is that you discover the joy and freedom that comes from the ability to enjoy activities in the company of just yourself. Feelings of fear may arise as you venture out alone, but courage and a feeling of a "job well done" will be the end results of your efforts. The confidence you will feel can liberate you from the frustration of being confined to your own home whenever you can't find another person to go out with you. Speaking for ourselves, we have always loved to take short trips individually. This allows us to stop when we please, eat when the mood strikes us, and enjoy long periods of silence for meditation, for journaling, and for soaking up the sights and sounds around us!

Getting to know and truly appreciate ourselves is the most rewarding outgrowth of our solitary forays into the outside world.

In the end, we are the only one who will never leave us; we are the only one who can be responsible for our mental and emotional health. However, reading about others' journeys on the road to self-discovery can be very helpful in developing and maintaining this type of psychological well-being. Authors such as Thoreau, Emerson, Victor Frankl, Clark Moustakas, and Marsha Sinetar share their stories and offer valuable suggestions in their works, telling readers how they might truly discover themselves. The process of getting to know and like ourselves, the process of learning to be our own best friend, is just that—a process. There is always room for more self-knowledge and more self-esteem. Don't give up on yourself. Start wherever you are, and begin to take the steps that will move you forward.

Of course, as vitally important as it is to be a friend to ourselves, we must also recognize the value of friendships with others. No doubt some women feel inadequate when it comes to extending themselves in friendship. If we haven't been in the habit of making friends easily, and if this is a practice that was formed way back in elementary school and even before, it takes will power and determination to change. Furthermore, if we have customarily been surrounded by family and a built-in support system in the past, we may not be skilled in reaching out for new friendships. Nonetheless, it is never too late to begin again. Probably the easiest way to make new friends is to do so in the context of shared activities and mutual interests. Many friendships, with both women and men, are formed in the workplace, in church groups, in clubs geared to different hobbies, and in adult education classes. Other possibilities include people we might meet while serving as a volunteer.

While you are in the process of reaching out and being open to new friendships, you will discover that many people will never be more than acquaintances, but others may be potential close friends. If you're at a point in your life where you want to make new friends, you will need to make some overtures. You will need to be able to risk rejection. One method might be to make a list of acquaintances you'd like to know better. Go down the list and invite each person to lunch.

You'll discover in the process that you want to know some of these people even better. Of course, it is sometimes the case that a person you want to know better may not want to pursue a closer relationship with you. It's important to avoid wallowing in feelings of rejection when another backs away. You can't be friends with everyone, and just because someone else doesn't respond to you doesn't mean that there's anything wrong with you; it may just mean that that person isn't right for your life at this particular time. If you're honest with yourself, you may realize that you have backed away from people at times, and perhaps they felt rejected. The more comfortable you are with yourself, the better able you are to handle these kinds of situations because you know that you are a valuable and worthwhile person regardless of someone else's opinion of you.

It's also helpful to remember that as you grow and change, not all of your friends will do so at the same rate. We have both found that some friends have dropped away over the years as mutual interests have faded. We have also come to realize that some people are not able to express their hurt or dissatisfaction with another, and so they simply withdraw. This can leave the other party baffled, wondering what happened. If your reasonable attempts to work out a reconciliation fail, there is nothing to do but release the other person and bless her or him, trusting that you will find friendships that are appropriate and comfortable for you. You don't have to stop caring about your friend who has chosen to withdraw from you; keep on caring about that person, but know that your lives will probably be separate from now on. Also be confident that you will attract other friends into your life.

There's a saying that "if you want a friend, be one." Be the kind of friend you'd want for yourself. Remember birthdays and special occasions. Be someone others can trust to keep confidences. Be there when needed. Don't be demanding and don't be a doormat. Be understanding as your friend grows and changes, and give support to that process. Be willing to communicate and to work out any misunderstandings. You'll find that any effort you put into making and keeping friends will be truly worth the effort.

The Perks of Being Alone

As we've seen, there are definite challenges involved in being a woman alone. However, there are also certain advantages. More and more women are choosing the single life because of these benefits. During the workshops that we have presented throughout the country, we have asked women of all races and religions and all walks of life to list what they like about being alone; inevitably, that list is at least as long as the one spelling out any disadvantages to aloneness. One positive point mentioned by many single women is that they have more time and energy to focus on career goals. A single woman need not take time out for bearing children or be concerned about a spouse's possible job relocation.

For example, White House correspondent Helen Thomas made the choice to stay single so that she could devote her time and energy to her career. She has been at the White House since Kennedy was President and has no regrets about remaining single for many years. At the age of 51 she met and married a fellow journalist but didn't change her lifestyle in the process; she couldn't tolerate any lack of independence. She enjoyed 11 years of marriage before her husband died. Because she knew how to function as a woman alone, she still leads a full and satisfying life in spite of being widowed.

Julie's life circumstances have been such that she's spent extensive periods of her life alone. While suffering through a certain amount of loneliness, she has also become aware of certain advantages to being alone. After a number of years of cooking and cleaning for husbands and children, it became a real treat to be able to choose to cook or not cook, to eat out with friends, or to just fix an egg or a sandwich and settle in with a good book some evenings. She found that all kinds of decisions became less of a hassle. She bought the car she wanted and felt she could pay for; she purchased the clothes she had her eye on without the need to justify the expense to someone else. In short, she went where she wanted, did what she wanted. She needed only answer to herself and found the freedom very gratifying.

There are those people who often perceive a single woman as lacking something, as someone who needs help. However, it is becoming ever more obvious that many single women choose to be single and, as exemplified by the full lives they live, they refute the negative stereotype. When Ione was teaching, she commented to a single older teacher whom she admired: "It's unfortunate that you don't have children of your own, since you are so wonderful with them." The woman replied very firmly, "Have you ever considered the possibility that I have chosen my single, childless life and that I'm quite happy just as it is?" For too long, many of us have assumed that if an older woman is single, it couldn't possibly be a matter of choice.

Not too long ago, we interviewed a beautiful and dynamic never-married lady who lives in a small town in Washington state. She shared her thoughts with us about her life and the choices she's made:

I had to develop myself and depend on myself from an early age because I was an only child. I didn't fully appreciate what it meant to be alone until I turned 40. I began to ask myself, "Is this healthy? 'Do I need anyone? Am I an Old Maid?" I'm learning to depend on myself more and more. My mother is dead, and my father lives in Florida, so my family unit is not in the next state. Before I moved here, I could get to my family in a day's drive. I'm now learning even more about getting my own identity.

I've always appreciated the freedom to come and go, to not have to compromise. I've been called selfish and have been asked, "Why can't you keep a man in your life? Why are you so hard to live with?" I'm not anti-child; I just prefer to be child-free. There is a difference. Research on child-free people shows that they haven't missed it, but we have few role models. I'm discovering it's okay; I'm not that strange after all.

When she spoke on ethics at an alternative high school, she shared information with the students on the various choices open to men and women with respect to parenthood. She didn't know how her talk would be received because the community is so conservative, but at this particular high school, the students were mesmerized. She was scheduled to be there 45 minutes, but stayed for two hours because the students couldn't stop asking questions and discussing the issues.

She describes herself and her single lifestyle:

I'm a queen bee, a networker. I live frugally; I'm a minimalist; I don't want to spend my life polishing furniture. I like straight lines, simple furniture; I eat well, take naps, have time for people. I appreciate rejuvenating energy exchanges. I keep toxic people out of my life; I don't want to gossip. Too many people are not making wise choices now.

Women especially have been programmed to accept limited choices. I've seen the result of this in the neighborhood where I grew up; there are too many women with their fourth child and their third husband. I go back and see that these people are into cooking and eating and another video. I feel there's more to life than a new car, the newest fashions, the newest concert. I want to develop more than that. I like to use my whole brain and think. I appreciate sun, rest, days of solitude. I know when to withdraw and when to be social.

I am human, so I am lonely at times, but I don't block it out because it is a time of growth. My advice to single women is don't get over-busy. Solitude is good. For a while, I went to every meeting and served on every board and that was ok, but there's more beyond that.

I find music to be a wonderful companion; it fills my inner landscape. I find that I do like myself. There are times when I feel no one on the planet understands me. Then I pick up a book and read or listen to a book on tape. I know the process is important, just to do what I'm led to do, and then just to be....

This dynamic and beautiful lady is an inspiration to those who come in contact with her, and she demonstrates the joy and richness of life that is possible for the single woman.

So, whether you find yourself alone by choice or not, for a short period of time or for longer stints, as you begin to look at the positive aspects of your situation and begin to take some constructive action, you will find that even your loneliness can be a vehicle for growth. As you learn to view this state from a new perspective, and as you explore some of the alternatives available to you, you will find that any loneliness you may feel from time to time will no longer have any real power over you.

We've spoken to many married women who would love to be doing all the things we've been talking about, but because of commitments to husbands and families, either they can't find the time, or spouses are too demanding or possessive to allow them much latitude. It has been said that marriage is like a bird in a cage. Those who are out want in, and those who are in want out. Instead of bemoaning our fate as single women, let's make the most of our lives no matter what our marital state. As single women, we can do what we want, and there is no need to be totally alone or lonely unless we choose to be. One thing is certain: There is a magnificent world full of things to do and to learn about; only the unwillingness to create a joyous and fulfilling life prevents a woman alone from achieving her dreams.

❖ SUMMING UP ❖

We all need and want love, support, and a degree of interaction with our fellow humans; we also need to learn how to be alone and how to appreciate our own company. In the final analysis, we are the only ones who will never leave us. We suggest that you review the options that we have presented in this chapter that can enrich the quality of your life and its very special and unique circumstances. Note the myriad alternatives for fulfilling your needs. If you make an effort to take advantage of these opportunities, you will find yourself more actively and joyously participating in the great adventure called Life. As a result, you will cease to feel victimized by loneliness. Why not begin that empowering process RIGHT NOW?!

Action Steps

◆ Make a list of the advantages of being alone.

◆ Invite someone you'd like to know better to lunch.

◆ Begin to write in a journal at least 10 minutes each day.

◆ Do or learn something new, perhaps something you've thought about but have never "gotten around to." This may involve attending a class or a workshop.

◆ Find a place to volunteer at least once a week.

◆ Research available support groups (at the YWCA, churches, women's centers, etc.), and make a commitment to attend at least six meetings.

◆ If you have other single friends, begin a support group for yourselves. (This book could be used as a starting point.)

◆ Read some of the books mentioned in the Recommended Reading list at the back of this book. Discuss them with at least one other person.

◆ Make a date to go out alone with yourself, and make a commitment to honor that date. Really make a point of being good to yourself. You might want to eat out at a favorite restaurant, attend a concert or play, or take a short trip—the particular activity is not important. Making the effort and enjoying yourself IS!

◆ Look in the mirror and affirm aloud each morning: *"I am a whole and complete woman, capable of experiencing happiness and fulfillment, no matter what my marital status. I now go out into my world with enthusiasm and optimism!"* (If you don't believe it the first time you say it, repeat it until you do!)

❖ ❖ ❖

BUILDING MUTUAL SUPPORT SYSTEMS

*"Each friend represents a world in us, a world possibly
not born until they arrive, and it is only by this meeting
that a new world is born."*

— Anaïs Nin

We have examined many of the ways that women alone can
fill their lives with companionship and camaraderie, and
now we turn our attention to the issue of living alone. Without question, some women truly appreciate living alone—that is, they relish
the freedom involved in coming and going as they please without
any questions asked and enjoy living in a household that is run just
as they wish it to be. They participate in many of the activities
we've discussed and do not view living alone as a hindrance to their
rich, fulfilling lives. Rather, they see their alone time as a precious
gift and actually prefer their solitary state. Many women engage in
mystical or spiritual practices, such as meditation and prayer, that
actually requires a certain amount of solitude, so living alone works
well for them. These women have resolved their issues, at least for
the present, so the lifestyle they have created for themselves is the
perfect choice for them.

However, although there are many among us who value our quiet
times in which we can reflect and take care of various and sundry
day-to-day responsibilities, we may not necessarily wish to live
totally alone for many of the reasons we have discussed earlier. We

are the women who are delving into, and endeavoring to create, alternative methods to fulfill our needs, and who are experiencing genuine joy and fulfillment in spite of deeply ingrained cultural expectations. We share with you now our personal experiences, as well as some innovative ways in which other women are building a deeply satisfying life.

Shared Lives / Separate Space

Before you take the initial steps toward experimenting with alternative living situations, it is best to first appraise your own needs and desires carefully. Engaging in some of the activities suggested earlier will give you a feeling of belonging and fellowship, a sense of just how many caring people there are in the community where you live. Since your participation will enable you to encounter some of the same people again and again, you will soon fashion a network of like-minded acquaintances from which you can begin to form friendships.

Some women find companions who also live alone, and together they build their own support groups. In fact, they function as extended families for one another and regularly share meals, participate in similar hobbies, create discussion groups, and enjoy various forms of entertainment together—both in and outside the home. They listen to each other's problems, give each other help when needed (assisting each other with transportation, plant- and pet-sitting, grocery shopping, and so much more), and generally advise and encourage one another.

Recently, there was an article in our local newspaper profiling a woman who had faked terminal breast cancer for two years. She shaved her head and purposely lost a great deal of weight to fool a cancer support group she was attending. Over a two-year period, the woman built a network of close friends among the members of the group and elicited the empathy and warmth she so desperately desired. It's a shame that she felt compelled to feign a life-threatening illness in order to receive the attention she so obviously craved in her loneliness, but this case points out how important it is to reach out to others.

Perhaps it's time for us to be more sensitive to our fellow human beings, to stop applying so much of our energy to the desperate search for a marriageable partner, and instead, use more of our energy in support of one another. Love, pathos, and a sympathetic ear should not be reserved only for women fighting life-threatening illnesses. We need to continually be aware that when women support each other, it does not lessen the possibility of marriage for those alone; it just makes life much more fulfilling, regardless of one's current or future marital status.

One group of older women that we know of who had fears and anxieties about living alone worked out a system in which they make a point of phoning each other at specified times each day. This practice ensures that each woman in the group receives a call two or three times every day, and it eliminates the possibility that anyone will lie injured or sick without help. If a woman is not going to be home to answer her phone at the specified time, she lets her phone friends know. Then if her phone remains unanswered for some time, the caller will personally check up on her friend.

This procedure may seem cumbersome, but for elderly people it can really work out. Ione's mother-in-law once lay helpless in her bathtub for 18 hours. The call button she wore around her neck had malfunctioned. As wonderfully effective as electronic devices are, they are not without their flaws, and nothing is really as comforting as the knowledge that someone cares.

Two women we know, one in her mid-forties, the other in her mid-fifties, have found the perfect way to live alone, but never be lonely. Both women are divorced professionals with their own homes, and one is the mother of an adult son. A few years ago they became acquainted, and over a period of time, became close friends. While each of the women continued to live in her own home, they shared most evening meals, provided each other with assistance in various and sundry ways, often took vacations together, and spent many entertaining and relaxing times in one another's company. They realized that they had created a mutually dependable support system that gave them both the extra strength they needed.

About two years ago, the younger of the women was offered a new job that was located 2,000 miles away from their hometown. The offer was too good of a career move to turn down, so it was with mixed emotions that the woman finally chose to accept the position. However, the two women had enjoyed such a warm and satisfying friendship that they decided to rise to this challenge by developing a way to keep their connection intact. To their delight, they found that, for a few years anyway, a strong friendship can survive a great distance. They telephone each other frequently, spend some of their vacation time traveling together, meet for long weekends as their schedules allow, and still try to "be there" for one another. When the older of the women is eligible for early retirement in a few years, she will move to the city where her friend now lives.

When we last talked with them, they were planning to buy a home together on the coast. They intend to rent it out for the time being and let it pay for itself, and eventually they will occupy it together. Both women find that they delight in engaging in many of the same activities, they enjoy the same types of people, and they thoroughly enjoy each other's company. These are benefits neither experienced in their marriages, and they've come to treasure happiness where they find it instead of continuing to search for some elusive dream.

A woman from Spokane, Washington, told us about developing a community for mutual psychological and spiritual support. All members of this community live in their own homes at various locations across the city, but they come together one evening every two weeks in a large basement recreation room. They share a potluck dinner, and one person each time is in charge of selecting the evening topic and moderating the discussion. A wide variety of topics is covered, and the members of the group take turns functioning in the leadership role. The woman originally responsible for inviting the group to come together for the purpose of community acts as the coordinator. As various members of this community wish to present a topic or invite someone in to provide an experience for the group, they contact the coordinator, and she does the scheduling. Some meetings are left open for spontaneous discussions or for dealing with issues pertaining to the group or its individual members. (For further exploration of ideas about this type of community, we highly recommend the book, *A Different Drum,* by M. Scott Peck, M.D.)

What follows are some other ways in which women can share their lives, but maintain their freedom and autonomy.

Group Apartment / Condo Living

Condominium living has become more and more popular in recent years, and most condominium complexes consist of diverse people who come together by happenstance. However, groups of like-minded people do build small condo complexes and live separate but interdependent lives. This arrangement could provide an excellent opportunity for a woman alone to create a new extended family and to enjoy the company of many different types of people with interests that complement different aspects of her own life and personality.

For example, a church group in Washington, D.C., purchased an entire apartment building. Each person owns her/his own apartment, but the residents share common facilities where they hold potluck dinners, group meetings, and church activities. A group of ambitious women should have no problem instituting a similar living arrangement!

Private Mobile Home Parks

Another alternative for women would be for a group of people to buy a few acres of land zoned for a private mobile home park. (For example, a reasonably priced small park with 12 spaces for mobile homes was advertised in our own local paper.) Each person could meet her individual requirements with a mobile home, and a community facility could be erected to meet common needs. There really is no end to the possibilities for creating a nurturing, caring, surrogate family of unrelated individuals. For example, another recent newspaper article dealt with a fire that had destroyed a small trailer park in northern Idaho. The residents felt displaced, not only because they sustained the loss of their homes, but because they were no longer together as a group. There were 13 mobile homes in this small park, and the residents were like one big family who shared holidays and looked out for one another.

Duplexes

Duplexes are another fine way for women to share their resources. Ione knows of two single women who lived in the same apartment building, and as they became friends, they found that they were spending a great deal of quality time together. They

Building Mutual Support Systems 39

decided to pool their savings and make a down payment on a duplex. Each woman lived in one unit and made one-half the down payment. In this way, each could have her own space, decorated according to her individual taste, yet enjoy the feeling of permanent camaraderie. Since neither woman had the funds to purchase a house of her own, and since both women longed to own property, this proved to be an ideal solution.

After several enjoyable years of residing in the duplex, the women went to an attorney and drew up a legal document protecting one another in the event of the other woman's death. Each of the women left their share to family heirs, but no sale could ever be forced until the remaining person chose to sell, move, or had passed away. Both women felt that they had supported one another over the years in ways that their individual family members hadn't had the time or inclination to do; therefore, they wanted that sustenance to live on as long as the remaining woman desired to stay in her home. Only recently, Ione learned that these women, no longer able to care for their property, had sold their duplex and moved into the same retirement home. They still have their "own place" together, assisting one another and enjoying the warm companionship developed over years of friendship.

Land Cooperatives

An idea cropping up in certain parts of the country is the concept of land cooperatives. Many people, including single women, are evaluating their often-extravagant lifestyles and discovering how easy it is to get obsessed with purchasing bigger homes and more material goods. While they may possess the earning power to enjoy an opulent way of life, the pursuit of "the American Dream" can mean sacrificing time with growing or adult children and other relatives, intimacy with partners, and the time to simply relax and enjoy the fruits of one's labors in a leisurely fashion. The conclusion that many women in this situation come to is: It's time to simplify my life!

In Tallahassee, Florida, several members of the same church are going through such an evaluation process; they are thinking about selling their homes and developing a land cooperative where they would share resources and work together toward common purposes. The families have found space in a modest, old neighborhood. They are planning on 16 individuals or families purchasing two-and-one-half acres of land. Everyone will build a modest home facing a central area that will be a car-free, safe haven. They dream of constructing a common building so that people may cook and eat together if they wish to do so. They want to recruit people of all ages and hope to engage in shared activities such as gardening, composting, recycling, and much more.

The ideas being implemented by people developing land cooperatives are varied. Some are urban land cooperatives, and some are rural, but they all have some basic underlying purposes. Two of the rural cooperatives that have been working for a period of time are the Miccosukee and Grassroots Land Cooperatives in Tallahassee. In these two cooperatives, the families share common ideals about environmental issues and about the importance of nurturing children, and they are willing to share responsibility for community activities, as well as for projects of global concern.

The country of Denmark has well over 100 such projects that have worked well and are termed "cohousing." They all originated with an idea, and then progressed to the completion stage through the efforts of a number of determined people who participated in the planning and building of these cooperatives.

If women alone would think creatively about their needs and what they really want from life, they too could create an enriching and supportive environment. There are women who would enjoy being a part of a land cooperative whether it involved only single people, just women, or families and individuals of all ages. It could start with just a few people but allow for expansion, as necessary. An article in the local newspaper inviting people to come together to explore the idea might be a good way to begin. People already meeting in a group for some specific purpose (church, environmental, personal growth, etc.) could form the basis for some type of cooperative effort. One thing's for sure: There are as many diverse ways of creating shared communities as there are people who wish to live in them!

Forming Long-Term Support Communities

In the early 1980s, several women formed a discussion group in Coeur d'Alene, Idaho. Most of the participants were in their late twenties or early thirties and were mothers of small children. Their purpose for meeting was to discuss pertinent issues of the day, to share family activities, and to support and encourage one another in the raising of their children. As time went by, the make-up of the original group was modified as some of the women left the area and new members joined. This second group has been together since 1986. They meet twice a month, participate in an annual summer campout that lasts four to five days, and make time for a three- to four-day winter retreat at one of the member's homes each year. In addition, they plan and take trips together from time to time.

Barbara Scarth, a member from the time of the group's inception, told us that the group has talked about purchasing a house so that single women from the group can live together. While many of the women are in happy, long-term marriages or partnerships, they are aware of the reality that as they get older, some of them might end up alone. It's interesting to note that even though some of the women thinking about investing in joint ownership of the home may never actually reside in it, they are willing to look out for the welfare of their fellow group members so that each person's future is secured in a very tangible manner!

Barbara's heartfelt sentiments about the group were evident as she told us: "The group is one of the most important parts of my life—no doubt about it! I can't imagine my life without it, or understand how anyone else can live without this kind of group for that matter!" Knowing Barbara over the past dozen years, we are aware of her deep commitment to her husband and children. She is certainly a solid and centered lady, so these statements do not come from a place of desperation or co-dependency, nor are they to be taken lightly. It's obvious that women such as Barbara are finding deep fulfillment in the various forms of community they are building.

Shared Housing / Shared Lives

As we've mentioned previously, many women truly fear the prospect of living alone. Some find it a financial drain, if not an impossibility. Some simply prefer to experience the emotional support and physical closeness of one or more individuals who live in the same household. For those women, a new trend is emerging, and many are finding shared homes and shared lives an enriching experience.

On the popular TV program, *The Golden Girls,* the late middle-aged to senior-citizen protagonists (Blanche, Rose, Dorothy, and Sophia) all shared Blanche's home in Florida. They each had separate jobs and interests, yet their lives were quite interdependent, and they provided each other with a great deal of strength and love. Many situation comedies of the past and present, such as *Full*

House, The Odd Couple, and *Designing Women* are examples of programs that have been built around people of diverse backgrounds who have come together to share their homes and lives.

A University of Florida gerontologist, Otto von Mering, calls this phenomenon the rise of the domestic unit and believes that shows such as *The Golden Girls* are reflecting a lifestyle that more and more older Americans are beginning to emulate. Mering points out that many more people are living to advanced ages— the 75 to 84 age group numbers 9.8 million and is 13 times larger than it was in 1900. This remarkable statistic means that older people need to create new ways to live, and it often necessitates finding methods through which they can extend limited retirement funds. Pooling resources is one way to do just that. Women, in particular, need to consider this option because, as a group, they account for 63 percent of the aging population. Also, women's salaries and retirement plans have amounted to much less, on the average, than that of comparable males, and since women make up 75 percent of the elderly poor, it's important that they find creative solutions that will allow for a quality life at every age. Many women are coming to a greater understanding of one another's needs and are entering into extended-family situations out of necessity. However, they are finding that such arrangements can provide rich emotional benefits, as well as solve problems of poverty and loneliness.

What follows are examples of women who have created unique alternatives to the living-alone issue.

Gladys and Jill—Early Role Models

Back in the 1950s, a woman named Gladys Taber wrote a monthly column in one of the popular women's magazines sold at the grocery checkout counter. In it, she often referred to

Stillmeadow, her New England estate, and she regularly mentioned her housemate, Jill. They had made the choice to live together years earlier when each had small children, and they formed their own unique family unit and support system during the Depression years. As unconventional as that living situation may have been for that era in history, it gives us a shining role model for the creative ways in which women of courage have solved the issue of aloneness in previous decades.

Paula—A Home Saved

A few years ago, a woman we know of named Paula almost lost the beautiful Victorian home she had grown to love. A change of jobs and a tight financial squeeze had caused her to fall behind in her mortgage payments. However, before she allowed herself to lose her home, she decided to rent out some of the rooms. The house contained four bedrooms plus a third story. Paula moved into the rooms on the third floor and placed an ad in the local paper for tenants.

There was immediate response to the ad, and Paula's screening process began. Some thought the rent was too high, but Paula defended the amount, saying: "You are paying not just for a room, but for a family." She had decided on some basic rules and would not allow smoking, children, or pets. As the screening of prospective renters continued, Paula saw that she had attracted the very people she had hoped to live with. Most were people in transition for reasons such as relationship breakups, job transfers, and other prosaic reasons. Some stayed a few weeks, and some a few months. There was a wide range of ages and occupations represented, and both male and female occupants were welcome. Common areas were for everyone's use, but bedrooms were considered strictly private.

One of the many benefits of shared arrangements like Paula's is that there is usually someone available if a person wants a companion for hiking, sharing a pizza, going to a movie, playing a board game, or just someone to lend a sympathetic ear. Sharing living arrangements can really be a blessing in some people's lives!

Gina and Gloria—Privacy and Companionship

Some women own their own homes and rent to others, but other women often decide to pool their resources and buy or build together. That way they can build a home to suit their unique lifestyle. Gina and Gloria pooled their resources and built a house with two bedrooms and a bath on each end. In the middle is a large living room, dining room, and kitchen. They share the middle rooms, and each woman has her own bedroom and bath, plus a guest room for any family or friends who might visit. Since their personal rooms are located at opposite ends of the house, they are not as likely to disturb one another with their varied hours and activities. They built the home after each was divorced and their children were raised. They decided on this arrangement when they were in their late forties; now well into their seventies, they are still reaping the benefits of their shared living arrangement.

Dorris and Pat—In Sickness and in Health

Dorris found herself alone after her children were raised and her husband had died a relatively early death. Pat never married and had lived with her mother and raised an adopted son, but she was now alone after her mother's death and her son's departure from the home. Pat and Dorris lived in the same small community, attended the same church, and had been casual friends over a long period of time. When Dorris's husband Roger became very ill, Pat provided sustenance and support. After Roger's death, the women continued their warm and mutually nurturing friendship. Whenever one of the women was suffering from an illness or recuperating from an accident of some sort, the other woman would move into that person's home, sometimes for weeks or months at a time. After a few years of this back-and-forth arrangement, the women decided it would be practical to live together. Pat first rented and then later sold her own home, used the money to build onto Dorris' home to add extra space and to accommodate her belongings, and then she moved in permanently. Each is secure in the knowledge that the other person will care for her when necessary, they occasionally travel together and, of course, they share household responsibilities. They have found that this arrangement works extremely well for them.

Kathryne and Roger—Beyond Age and Gender

Ione's cousin, Kathryne, found herself caring for Max, her terminally ill husband, a large home, and overwhelming outdoor landscaping. Max suggested that they let some deserving student use the third floor of their spacious home in return for the yard work and some other minor duties. Roger, a doctoral student working to put himself through school, seemed to fit the bill, so Kathryne and Max allowed him to move in, which permitted him to quit work and finish his doctorate.

Soon after Roger moved in, Max died. Kathryne continued to need help, and Roger supplied the added muscle to keep the large home and grounds going. Although Roger is many years younger, has his own job and interests, and may soon have to leave to pursue his career, he has continued to rent his upstairs quarters. He and Kathryne have become friends, sharing an avid interest in the arts and enjoying many of the same activities. Kathryne has not had to ramble around in a huge home herself and has been able to do a lot of traveling, with the secure knowledge that her home is in good hands. Roger has found comfortable living quarters as well. This is just another example of a shared living arrangement that is mutually beneficial for both parties on many levels.

Clarabell and Harriet—Short-Term Sharing

Clarabell is a widowed artist getting along in years who found herself being afraid to live alone. Her children are all married and comfortably involved with their own families. She heard about a program at the local university where artists could support students in the school's art program by giving them a place to live. Clarabell signed up, and Harriet, a divorced, middle-aged student with grown children, moved in with her for a two-year period while completing her master's degree in art. This arrangement provided Clarabell with companionship, alleviated her fear of staying alone at night, and it helped Harriet obtain her objective. It also allowed Clarabell to stay in her own home two years longer than might have otherwise been possible.

Other Alternatives

Another recently widowed friend has a lovely home overlooking the Columbia River Gorge. She loves where she lives and did not want to consider moving, so her creative alternative was to convert her home into a bed-and-breakfast inn. This option allows her to remain in her beautiful and comfortable surroundings while enjoying the companionship of her patrons.

We also know of a divorced woman living in Southern California who would like to find someone in the Pacific Northwest with whom to share seasonal housing. Her goal is to spend two or three summer months out of the California heat. In return, the other person would spend some of the cold winter months basking in the California sunshine. When this woman is ready to retire, she plans to run an ad in the local newspaper of the city or cities of her choice and try to effect this arrangement.

If you would like to consider house sharing, but don't know of anyone else seeking to do so, begin putting out feelers among your friends or putting ads in your church or community group newsletter, in your local newspaper, at the YWCA, or at your nearest women's center. This idea is gaining tremendous popularity, so it will probably not be too long before you find a suitable partner.

There are also organizations that are beginning to crop up that help people find appropriate house-sharing arrangements. One such organization for older people is Housing Alternatives for Seniors, in Santa Monica, California. They report that most of the thousands of "matches" they've made have been very successful. Another place for information is the National Shared Housing Resource Center. (They may be contacted at 431 Pine Street, Burlington, VT 05401, or by calling 802-862-2727.) It's important for us to remember that service organizations appear in response to our needs. If enough people begin calling the various groups we've mentioned, plus the local Chamber of Commerce, more services such as Alternative Housing may be formed for the benefit of all age groups. Sitting back and feeling sorry for ourselves accomplishes nothing. We empower ourselves by taking responsibility and then taking action!

Individual Differences—Individual Decisions

When considering shared living arrangements, women need to exercise caution, and they need to be clear in their thinking. If you are in transition or believe you might only require short-term accommodations, it's better to rent from someone or, if you own a house yourself, to rent to others. In this manner, mobility is more easily assured. However, if you are looking for more permanence, you might wish to seek out a person who has the same goals and then pool resources and ownership of a living space.

It's important to remember that there are as many arrangements as there are people to make them. Honest communication on each person's part, plus solid research with respect to financial and legal issues, helps ensure a mutually satisfactory lifestyle for everyone. As in all marriages and nuclear families, there will, no doubt, be problems that arise that had not been taken into account prior to sharing a living situation. However, just about any problem can be solved if both parties are willing to sit down and talk and work towards a reasonable solution. So, if you truly do not choose to live alone, try not to let your fear of potential difficulties prevent you from entering into a life-enriching arrangement. If, on the other hand, you know deep in your heart that you are too set in your ways to compromise with another person or to honestly communicate, it's best to choose a lifestyle that is more in line with your temperament, needs, and personality. If you're honest with yourself, if you trust your intuition, and if you don't let anyone talk you into anything you're not entirely comfortable with, you are certain to select the lifestyle that is just right for you!

Julie's Hawaii Story

One of the most beautiful and satisfying episodes of my life came about as the result of a painful experience. I was teaching in Michigan at the time, my teenage daughter was living with her father and stepmother, and I had been feeling lonely for several months. Consequently, I entered into a hasty and unwise marriage. After a few months, it became apparent that I had placed myself in a miserable situation that no amount of counseling could fix. We divorced, but my ex-husband was a fellow faculty member who not only continued to harass me at work, but also proceeded to interfere in every aspect of my life. I was emotionally very shaken and actually considered suicide.

The turning point came when, in the midst of my despair, my friend Linda came to visit me from Hawaii. During the course of that visit, I shared my predicament involving my ex-husband with her, and she suggested that I visit her and her sister Connie for the summer. My first thought was that such a visit would be too much for me to arrange.

However, that night I dreamed about being in Hawaii and woke up with the idea that I might not only go there for the summer but perhaps for an extended period if my friends had room to accommodate me. The sisters were willing; I was granted a year's leave of absence, and I sold some investment property, my car, and my mobile home to finance my trip.

As it turned out, I was not the only one who was making hasty decisions. Connie picked me up at the Honolulu airport and broke the news that she had a new husband and that Linda would soon be moving to Maui with her boyfriend. They assured me that I could stay with them until I found other arrangements and that they would introduce me to people and help me find a suitable place to stay. They knew some transcendental meditation (TM) devotees (the sisters and I faithfully engaged in this practice) who lived in a group home in a lovely mountainside neighborhood overlooking downtown Honolulu. They were looking for another person to share their living arrangements, so my friends took me over to meet them. I was favorably impressed with the house and with the men and women who lived there. The common bond among us was the desire for spiritual growth and the commitment to meditate regularly. They invited me to move in, and I accepted. My share of the rent and utilities turned out to be incredibly reasonable, and I breathed a sigh of relief.

Each of us had our own room (with a shared bath), and the rest of the house was open to all. Each housemate was responsible for his or her own meals, and we each had a shelf in one of the refrigerators. We were all of different ages and at varying stages in our lives: George and Jennie were the oldest, both a little younger than I was, both divorced with children who occasionally visited. Kurt was a Vietnam vet who was attending law school at the University of Hawaii. Lorraine, Janna, Sally, and Howie all worked or were in school. Despite the differing backgrounds and circumstances, we were all compatible, and the house ran smoothly. I shared beach time, movies, and other outings with my new friends, and I never felt lonely. I knew there would always be someone to talk to if I felt the need. At the same time, I had as much time for myself as I wanted. The best of both worlds!

It was during this important time in my life that I re-learned something I'd forgotten since growing up with my brothers: Men could be friends without the complication of possible sexual entanglements. Due to my sense of loneliness, I'd slipped into the habit of looking at most men I met as "possibles"—as potential dates or husbands. Living in this community atmosphere helped me regain a more balanced relationship with men.

Another bonus came along during this time. My daughter Colleen graduated from high school back in Michigan and went to live in Colorado with her boyfriend. After I'd been in Hawaii for a few months, she called and confessed that her relationship wasn't working out and that she didn't know what to do. I invited her to come to Hawaii so that we could work on the problem together. My room in the house was very spacious, and there was no objection to my sharing it with my daughter. All we needed to do was pay her share of the utilities. When Colleen arrived, she decided to learn to meditate and to join in the spirit of the house. She easily made friends with the others, and the two of us reconnected as adults and friends in a very special way that benefits us even now, years later. She stayed seven months and then came back to Michigan with me, enrolled in the college where I was teaching, and lived with me for the next three years.

This experience in community living was a life-changing one for me. It healed my wounded psyche and provided an atmosphere of safety and joy that allowed me the opportunity to learn and grow and eventually make wise decisions that have enriched my life in myriad ways. A word of caution, however: When entering into a community situation, you need to be reasonably confident that the group's values are compatible with your own. I believe my Hawaii experience turned out well despite age differences and varied backgrounds and occupations because we shared a commitment to spiritual growth and meditation. Community living requires making adjustments and compromises, as well as the willingness to work out problems on a daily basis. If there are common values among the members of the group, the likelihood increases that the arrangement will work out to everybody's satisfaction.

❖ SUMMING UP ❖

Creating expanded family units is one positive way to eliminate loneliness and overcome our fears of spending the rest of our lives alone. Whether we share our lives while living in separate homes or choose to share both our lives and living quarters, we can develop a warm and loving support system. Many people are already involved in doing just that—AND YOU CAN BE, TOO!

Action Steps

◆ Sit down quietly, and think of examples from your own experience where people have lived together in extended-family (related or nonrelated) units.

◆ If you think of any people currently involved in alternative-living arrangements, invite them over for an evening and ask them to share their experiences with you.

◆ Call one or two friends who are single and ask them to share an evening exploring ways in which they might be interested in temporarily creating a mutual support system.

◆ Form a group of singles (two or more), and plan on engaging in one or more of the following activities on a regular basis:

a) read and discuss a book

b) dine out

c) go to movies or plays

d) take a class together

e) share in a craft or hobby

f) watch or participate in sporting events

g) explore psychological and spiritual growth

◆ Attend a group that has already been formed at a local church, YWCA, women's organization, or other community center.

◆ Form a group of two or more women to read about and explore the various alternatives for women alone presented in this book.

◆ Affirm often: *"I now attract the perfect people into my life for the purpose of creating a loving and nurturing mutual support system."*

❖ ❖ ❖

CHAPTER THREE

BUILDING THE HOLO COMMUNITY

"Once a group has achieved community, the single most common thing members express is: 'I feel safe here.'"

— M. Scott Peck, M.D.

The building of the Holo Community is our personal adventure into that arena of shared lives and shared housing we've just discussed. People are always curious about when and how we came together to build and develop both a common life and a common ministry. As with most things, it has been a step-by-step process that has evolved with time and circumstance. Since life is ever-changing, our community has needed to be fluid enough to allow for the varying needs of its participants. This has not always been an easy task, but we try to remain open to learning and absorbing more and more each day, and to seize the opportunities to grow personally and spiritually when challenges arise. We now present you with a look into the life of the Holo Community as it has evolved and as it currently functions.

Beginnings—Ione's Story

One of the biggest decisions of my life came to fruition in 1980, but only after a great deal of inner struggle and several years of incubation. I had been married for 26 years to a kind and wonderful man. We had raised two fine sons, and the youngest one was about to enter his last year in high school. My husband, Ace, was, and still is, a fine minister in a very small town in Oregon with a population of about 500. The nearest city of any size is Portland, a hundred-mile drive to the west down the Columbia River Gorge. Ace is a real shepherd to his flock and extremely happy in his chosen work. He is exactly where he needs to be, and I lived in that small town with him for nine years. However, in order to do so, I gave up my own career in an educational system and moved from a stimulating academic and cultural milieu to a community with no real opportunities for me. I used those years to read, to learn, to grow spiritually, and to raise our two boys. Nevertheless, I always knew deep inside of me that when the boys left home there wasn't going to be much left for me to do in that limited environment.

My husband and I were never real companions. He was, and still is, a loner in many respects. While he enjoyed dealing with people as part of his work, when he was not engaged in his ministerial duties, he preferred to spend most of his time by himself. Also, we didn't really share a passion for the same outside pursuits. He liked sports, but disdained travel, theater, music, workshops, personal growth groups, and all the interests that nourished my soul. For the first 17 years of our marriage, we had lived near larger cities, so I either had family or single professional friends who were willing to participate with me in the "great adventure of life." Ace never minded that I engaged in these activities; however, once we had moved a hundred miles from a city and into such a small farm community, the abundance of opportunities and stream of stimulating people flowing in and out of my life came to an abrupt halt. I did take some evening classes and workshops in Portland, but the 200-mile round trip kept those excursions to a minimum. I also drove or flew greater distances for certain activities, which helped.

But ultimately, having no one to really share the day-to-day process with creates deep loneliness in one born with a need for meaningful dialogue and deep personal and spiritual intimacy. So, after acknowledging all my fears and weighing all my alternatives, I chose to begin the preparations to move my life in another direction after our youngest son's graduation. I want to emphasize that I did not leave because my husband was "wrong" in some way, nor did I feel guilty about changing the course of my life; I simply made the decision to stop playing the traditional role of the "grin and bear it" wife.

My good friend Masil (who was growing discontented with her marriage for her own reasons) and I decided we wanted to build a healing community. In 1980 we sought inner direction about where to locate and were led to Northern Idaho. We found five acres of wooded property north of Coeur d'Alene, immediately fell in love with the land, and made an offer to buy. In a few days, we were the owners, and a new phase of life had begun. During the winter of 1980 to 1981, we drew up plans for a 13-room home. The following spring we returned to Idaho and planted an orchard and an asparagus bed, located an architect and contractor, and by June 1st, the day after my youngest son graduated from high school, we loaded trucks and cars and started the 300-mile trek to Idaho. Only a few days later, earth-moving machinery began to dig the foundation for the Holo Center.

Masil and I lived in a small camper during the initial construction period that first summer. It was an exciting time as we explored the area and got acquainted with neighbors and other local residents. We watched the backhoe operator dig away the excess soil from the hill that would allow us to build into the bank and have a partially earth-sheltered home. My husband helped us put a large barrel (which we painted black to absorb the sun's rays) high up on poles to enable us to have a solar shower. To our dismay, we soon discovered that the water that came out of the shower head was always very cold. We finally concluded that our idea of a solar shower was impractical. We had filled the barrel full of water, and since the temperature drops drastically at night in northern Idaho—down to 60 degrees or below—the water could not get sufficiently warm during the day. With 12 or more hours of cool weather at night, and with abnormal seasonal cloudiness and rain that summer, the solar energy just wasn't able to do the job.

Desperate for a warm bath, we went to our local K-Mart and picked up a child's swimming pool. We filled it with water, placed it in the sun and, generally, it warmed sufficiently for a bath under the pine forest on our land. If it didn't, a bucket of boiling water heated on the propane burner in the camper was enough to give us a comfortable bath. We began to differentiate between illusion and reality, between dreams and practicality! We had become pioneers in our own way. We still had enough of the dreamer in us to press forward, and yet enough sense to let go and revamp without beating our heads against brick walls. We were learning!

Since it was a very wet summer, we became accustomed to the frustrations of intermittent progress in the construction. Even on the days when it was sunny, we had to deal with contractors who only showed up sporadically. However, the slowed construction gave us time to enjoy the quiet of the small camper and the screen tent we had put up under the trees. The screen tent allowed us to sit outside even in the gently falling rain, and we truly were able to enjoy the fragrance of the pine trees and the beauty of our land. The screen tent also served as a place to store those extra items that did not fit into the camper or the canvas tent that housed tools and other essential belongings.

We cooked many meals in the camper, but we also discovered many of the fine restaurants in the area. As the rain continued week after week, going out to dinner gave us a break from long evenings in the camper and afforded us contact with other people. It was a wonderful summer, both as it was happening and now, in retrospect.

By August we had moved into a huge 3,000-square-foot shell. Armed with books, tools, questions, and enthusiasm, the two of us (aged 46 and 58 at the time) started to build the 13 rooms of the interior. Neither of us had ever done anything like this before, but we soon learned that this task wasn't unlike the sewing we had done as homemakers. Different tools and materials were involved, but essentially we just measured, cut, and fastened it together. We discovered that carpentry, once thought to be exclusively in the male domain, was suddenly demystified. It really wasn't that difficult. Because we didn't have the brute strength that some males possess, it was necessary to do some things more creatively. Although it took the two of us working cooperatively to put up a panel of wood or sheet rock, we could easily do it if we worked together. We reminded ourselves that even strong men come to the end of their strength and have to rely on one another or on machines. We merely had to do it sooner in some cases.

When we weren't certain how to proceed with some project, we bought books or asked lots of questions at the local building supply store. The employees were very gracious about answering our questions and extremely helpful to us, often contributing additional tips or information we hadn't thought about. Three workers, Bart, Wes, and Jim, became enthusiastic about our project and often inquired about our progress when we visited the store. They managed to overcome their initial surprise and reservations about two women finishing the entire interior of a house by themselves. As their respect grew, they schooled us in using the proper construction vocabulary and became increasingly supportive in every phase of our building program.

It was uncanny how help would appear just at the right moment. When we were puzzling over how to proceed with the diagonal walls that we wanted in the living and dining areas, our dear friends Milt and Sally Osborn pulled in the driveway. They lived 350 miles away, but they were out exploring in their motorhome and decided to stop in and spend a few days helping us. Milt was a retired carpenter, so he was able to show us how to cut the diagonal boards and where to begin placing them. Satisfied that we had learned that particular skill, he then moved on to something else. He also helped us put up sheet rock and taught us how to tape and finish the seams. After a week, Milt and Sally left us on our own, but with several new skills under our belts.

To complete the entire project, which included installation of cedar siding and the entire interior of the house, we only hired one carpenter for one day! After putting in the windows, we weren't certain how to level the sills and finish the area around them. We told the carpenter that we wanted to hire him for one day to show us how to finish one, and then we'd like him to supervise while we completed one. He agreed, and we learned the mechanics of one more building skill. So month after month and board after board, we worked away on our 13-room project.

Both Masil and I experienced immense satisfaction as we worked with the redwood, cedar, and knotty pine. We lovingly blessed every phase of our construction, every board we nailed in place. We prayed that this endeavor might be filled with love and healing so that everyone who came to our new home might feel those vibrations emanating from the very walls themselves.

Seven months later, we laid down our hammers, unplugged the radial arm saw, and stood back and marveled at our handiwork.

We had mastered many new building skills, learned even more about carpentry, and had even gotten the knack of pounding nails straight! I still marvel at the faith we must have had to undertake such a seemingly overwhelming project without any experience at all, but we just took it one day at a time, and the amazing result is that we're immensely proud of the quality of our work!

Building Additions

Four years after the completion of the initial phase of our work, we added a large 18- by 24-foot solarium onto the front of the house. It faces south and gives us some passive solar heating in the winter. Since the rest of the house is partially earth sheltered, we needed one room with a great deal of light, and we all spend a lot of time in that most pleasant of rooms.

During the summer of 1990, nine years after we began our original building, we added a wing to the house that contains an indoor heated year-round swimming pool. This very well might be the final addition. We have talked about literally raising the roof and adding extra bedrooms and bathrooms upstairs, but we have put that project on indefinite "hold." We need to take the time to discern what is feasible for the future. We are growing older, so the amount of time and energy and money we have left may need to be devoted to other pursuits.

For one thing, we have decided that a furnace is a must. We came to Idaho to build a healing community that would, among other things, encompass the ideal of self-sufficiency. For the past 13 years, we have heated with wood gleaned largely from an additional five acres purchased in 1988. A substantial Blaze King catalytic stove heats the main part of the house quite adequately, and a large fireplace containing an insert is the main source of heat for the solarium.

A few years ago we put in some electric heaters that give us the freedom to be away from the house for a few days at a time. However, electric heat is not efficient and is too expensive for our large home in a northern climate. Wood heat is comfortable, but it takes a great deal of effort to cut, split, haul, and stack the wood. Then, it all has to be carried to the house again during the long winter months, and oftentimes, it has to be split yet again to fit into the stove. While carrying out this task is certainly good exercise, we do have to consider how long we will physically want to undertake such a monumental chore. There is wisdom in preparing for one's eldership while one is in good shape to do so! So, within the next year or two, we will be putting in central heating. Sometimes, the dream has to be altered to fit the reality. Yet, we're certain we will continue to burn our wood stoves for many years to come (as long as they are environmentally sound), but a furnace definitely gives us options, and that is important to all of us.

Holo Center Ministry

The word *Holo* is from the Greek word for *whole,* and from the first moment that Masil and I conceived of building the Holo Center, our intent was to create a loving and safe place where people could come to work toward integration. We dreamed of a ministry that would nourish the whole person, where learning and healing in all its myriad forms—physical, emotional, and spiritual—could occur. That dream has been realized.

We (Masil, Julie, and Ione) are collaborators on the pathway to awakening. We believe in the multidimensional potential of humankind and believe that there is much more to life than can be perceived by the five senses. We always try to be open to our higher selves and to the information that can be accessed from that

source. We always look toward the positive, toward taking responsibility for feelings and attitudes, and toward understanding that the
choices we make create our lives. Since we believe that we are
comprised of body, mind, and spirit, we employ a variety of techniques to help people find that connection and reach their full
potential.

Over the years, we have welcomed a variety of men and women
for both short- and long-term sharing. Our friend Lucretia took a
"time-out" from her career as an attorney and lived with us for a
nine-month period while she regrouped and rethought her life during the summer of 1982 until the spring of 1983.

Julie joined us in December of 1982 and lived at the center for
five-and-a-half years. During that time, we purchased a motorhome
and traveled around the United States for two-and-a-half years conducting workshops and seminars on a variety of subjects. In June of
1988, Julie moved to Tallahassee to take on a church ministry. In
June of 1991, she returned to the center to live, and we are now
engaged in writing and self-publishing. Julie has completed her
autobiography, entitled *From Soap Opera to Symphony,* a book
about her struggle with adversity, her survival, and how she has
used her experiences to help others. Ione has completed a book,
*Empowering the Child from Within: Education and Parenting for
the Twenty-First Century,* which is full of innovative yet practical
ideas for parents, teachers, and others who interact with children. [1]

Masil's Insights

The sharing of insights on our community life would be incomplete without giving Masil a chance to express a few of her
thoughts. When we asked her to comment on what she saw as the
most important aspect of community life, she replied without hes-

---

[1] Either of these books can be purchased for $12.95 plus $3.00 postage by
writing to us at E. 955 Grand Tour Drive, Hayden, Idaho 83835. For a brochure
on the Holo Center, please mail a self-addressed stamped envelope to the
Hayden address above.

itation, "Sharing one another's lives—the working and playing together and basically creating our own family unit. Our shared lives provide many areas of growth. As we interact and react, we learn about ourselves and our subpersonalities, and then that enables us to make better choices about how we would like to respond."

When we discussed the issue of aging, Masil went on to say, "I take comfort in feeling like a family. Knowing that I would care for either Ione or Julie if they needed it and feeling they would do the same for me should the tables be turned, is a source of comfort for me. There is a certain concern or awareness of one another's welfare that makes you not feel alone. It's nice to be 'graying' together."

Masil feels a special connection for the land and constantly cares for and beautifies it. "I especially love our home and land, which sits in a more rural setting. I enjoy the harmony of the birds, of all the wild animal life and wildflowers that share our life and land. I've always felt that if we see the beauty in the natural world, then we can know that it reflects the harmony and beauty within ourselves. It brings us closer to experiencing our totality. Our community affords us the opportunity to experience ourselves in many ways, and I am happy we decided to build it!"

Julie's Story

I came to the Holo Center in December of 1982 after the major building project was finished. After living in Michigan for many years, I'd come to Idaho for what I thought would be a great new adventure. Two years earlier, I'd left my tenured position as a college professor of English to attend ministerial school in preparation for a completely new phase of my life. When I was presented with the opportunity to be the minister of a Unity church in northern Idaho, I was pleased and excited. It was at that church that I met Ione and Masil.

After being in the academic ivory tower for 11 years, the demands and pressures of that particular ministry left me dismayed and exhausted. Although I'd just spent two years in school preparing for just about any circumstance that might arise, I still wasn't prepared for the difficulties that I encountered. It only took me a few short months to realize that I was not happy and that I needed to regroup.

It was then that Ione and Masil, who had become dear and supportive friends, invited me to come and live at the center and help with their counseling and retreat ministry. My first order of business was to rest and recuperate physically, emotionally, and spiritually. It wasn't long before I realized that as much as I thought I'd healed my past and finished my inner business before I went to ministerial school, I had merely scratched the surface. There was much more to deal with. I had allowed the shame I felt about my beginnings and about certain past behaviors to rule. I'd pasted some very good truth principles over it all, but the core issues were still there to be dealt with. I was in the perfect place to begin my deep healing process.

Through methods such as rebirthing and other types of inner healing, I worked through the trauma and degradation of early childhood sexual abuse and neglect and the frustration and shame associated with being the daughter of an alcoholic and then the wife of two of them. I hadn't sufficiently grieved the death of my oldest son Richard, nor had I acknowledged the pain and disillusionment I felt when I tried to mother my epileptic, emotionally disturbed second son. There were so many dysfunctional elements in my life that it truly seemed like a melodramatic soap opera. I had managed to climb out from it and become a successful professional, but the infrastructure of my psyche was in dire need of attention and repair.

In the Holo Center atmosphere of unconditional love and acceptance, a place where many specific psychological and spiritual skills could be utilized, I began to heal at deeper and deeper levels. For the first time, I was able to fully comprehend and appreciate the concept of the "wounded healer." Because I'd undergone so many trials myself and had come out on the other side, I could be a compassionate and discerning guide for others who were prepared to do the necessary inner work that would effect their healing.

The many men and women who have come to the center for healing work and the scores of people we've worked with in our workshops have allowed me to see that my problems and circumstances are not entirely unique. Countless people have incredible stories and massive amounts of "soap opera" stuff to work through. So many of us here in Earth School have managed to get caught up in our dramas of pain and suffering. I feel extremely privileged to be in a position where I can use my own personal experiences in a way that will not only advance my soul growth, but which can help others learn and grow using their own life script.

This opportunity has been made possible for me because the Holo Community has been a safe and nurturing place to live and work. I did take a "time out" for three years to minister in a Unity church in Tallahassee, Florida. It turned out to be a very positive and healing experience for me, one that allowed me to "finish business" and erase the sense of failure I had carried over from the unfortunate experience in my first church ministry.

Living in the Holo Community does not excuse me from continual work on the spiritual and emotional path, however. We are all still in the process of working toward radiating 100 percent unconditional love 100 percent of the time. We're not there yet. Community life presents many opportunities to release controlling behavior, to forgive those who have previously injured us, and to let go of past programming, so we're all learning and growing and making mistakes together, and we are grateful for the opportunity.

Discussions and Explorations

Good communication is always necessary whenever we work and live with other people. Through discussion and listening and a lot of give-and-take, it has been much easier for us to define our common purpose, which, for us, is individual independence and autonomy in the framework of a loving, caring, supportive community. When our buttons get pushed, which they inevitably do, we retreat to the quiet of our own inner place and measure what has happened in the light of what our purpose is and in the light of what we value. We know that love is not always doing or being what someone else wants, for we cannot be healthy and wear the persona that someone else hands us. Nonetheless, we do attempt to be loving in all situations. Even when we have to set strong personal boundaries, we are learning to be both loving and assertive.

We have also found it helpful to discuss what work is necessary in order to meet our basic needs and then divide the tasks. The essential chores are handled in this way, but after that is done, each person has the freedom to select other activities that fulfill her own needs or desires. Communities take many forms, but effective communication and a sincere desire to share one's life with others must be the motivating forces if community living is to succeed.

Intensive Retreats

Individuals, couples, or small groups can arrange to live with us at the Center for a week or more to work in-depth on their specific personal growth processes. We work two to three hours a day for five days. We begin the first day by sitting down together to decide where the person, couple, or group feels they are emotionally and spiritually and what benefits they would like to derive from their stay. We listen attentively to their story and then coordinate a program that will work most effectively for them. Individual sessions are held in the morning; we suggest various assignments to be done in the afternoons, and people are encouraged to explore our extensive library of books and tapes.

Fun and relaxation are also integral parts of the process. During the summer and winter months, we like to walk, go to movies, and attend plays, musical concerts, or other special events. When there's snow, we cross-country ski. In the summer, the surrounding lakes make a wonderful setting for swims and picnics. We welcome and encourage participation in all aspects of life in the community for the week, but our attendees are also free to spend as much time alone as they desire or to explore the surrounding area in small groups or by themselves. Intensive retreats are a rich experience for people seeking psychospiritual growth (psychological growth coordinated and blended with spiritual growth), and we appreciate the in-depth interaction and the lasting connections with other members of our human family.

Working Together in Community

A community can be a safe place from which to extend one's hands out into the world and still have a warm and loving base to come home to. There will always be those people who prefer to be more rooted and will spend most of their time at home. Others will choose to be more mobile.

We have found that some of the marked advantages of community as we have developed it, are the pooling of resources, including money, talent, and energy. What one person cannot afford to do alone becomes more feasible when others are also contributing, and since we all have different talents and a variety of interests, a multiflavored dimension is added to our group living.

Masil is a registered nurse who loves the outdoors. She cultivates beautiful flowers, trees, and produce. Both literally, and often figuratively, she keeps the home fires burning. Some years, she also serves as bookkeeper for the Center, and she will do her share of just about anything else that needs to be done. She is a whiz at repairs and creating solutions to problems that arise in the physical environment, be that house or land. We often lovingly refer to her as our "Ruby Goldberg"! Masil also took up oil painting after we moved to Idaho and has become quite masterful in her work. She sells both originals and prints of her art.

Julie was a college English and Composition professor. She has fine organizational skills and performs much of the public relations work for the Holo Center. She sets up the workshops that we (Julie and Ione) conduct throughout the country, and sends out and responds to most of the correspondence the Holo Center receives.

Ione has been an educator and counselor in the public school system, and she continues to be a spiritual therapist in our ministry. She cooks and plans most of our meals—we all help with the major housecleaning—and Ione assists Masil with outdoor tasks. Julie and Ione both write and create the informational and inspirational tapes that we have available, but it is Ione's responsibility to take care of the actual production of our products, such as duplicating the tapes.

Grace is Masil's mother and is 91 years young. She helps us to confront our own aging process and teaches us to be patient with her declining physical and mental capacities. She is usually mellow and retains a good sense of humor. She still goes up and gets the mail and newspapers in the morning and often washes the dishes after a meal. She likes to go to movies with us, but usually tells us afterwards, "They don't make them like they used to!"

The three of us (Julie, Masil, and Ione) have many common threads running through our lives, and we feel it's no accident that we found ourselves living and working in community together. Masil and Julie both lost their oldest sons, suddenly and unexpectedly, within a month of each other in 1960. The boys were ten and nine years of age at the time. Each of them has a handicapped second son, and each has one daughter, born just a month apart. Julie was adopted at the age of nine, Ione adopted her youngest son at the age of nine, and all three of Masil's children are adopted. Even long before we had ever met one another, the events of our lives were weaving similar patterns.

Through community living, we have found the deep satisfaction that comes from the blending of our loved ones. We have each brought many beautiful friends, as well as our children, into this extended family unit, and all of our lives have been blessed by the intermingling of the people who come to be embraced, and who, in turn, embrace all of us.

We are succeeding in our attempts to add richness, caring, and support to one another's lives and individual journeys as well as to our collective journey. Each of us brings deep insights and clarity to one another. We do not mean to indicate that we never experience conflict. However, we do have the will to hang in there and find ways of pushing through the difficulties, and to see our own splintered personalities through the mirror image that the other person is holding up before us. Any problems that do arise actually amount to a very small portion of our total existence, and we are learning how to become collaborators on the pathway to personal and spiritual growth.

❖ SUMMING UP ❖

Being a woman alone does not necessitate being lonely or poor. Many wonderful alternatives are just waiting to be investigated, and there are myriad benefits to be derived from being single. Open your mind and heart to exploring them. Our intention in writing this chapter was to demonstrate how we, in the Holo Community, have found creative solutions to the often-challenging issues surrounding single women and to show that it is very possible to overcome emotional and physical stumbling blocks and to live a joyous and fulfilling life.

You can, too!

❖ ❖ ❖

CHAPTER FOUR

CREATING FINANCIAL INDEPENDENCE

*"You can build your wealth under any economic conditions
including inflation, recession, or even depression. It's what
you know and not what's happening around you that counts."*

— Charles J. Givens, author and financial consultant

At a very early age, boys are trained to begin thinking of ways to
become financially independent. During most of this century
(and all those preceding it) the notion has been culturally ingrained
that the man is the breadwinner who must provide for his family. A
girl has traditionally been given the subtle message to "just find
something to do" until the right man comes along to take care of
her. These long-established stereotypes are being challenged and
modified to some degree, but it takes a long time to eradicate such
deep-rooted programming—many decades (or even centuries) for
the collective unconscious to change.

Women have been striving for career advancements, for equal
pay for equal work, and for opportunities in professions formerly
held solely by men. Even though a significant amount of progress
has been made, statistics show that women still lag far behind men
in wage-earning ability. Many parents continue to believe that it's
more important to educate a boy, and they are more apt to assure
that their male child has an advanced education, or at least train-

73

ing in some skilled labor field. Parents often pass down the family business or set the son up in a business of his own. They may consider and plan for these possibilities while the boy is still very young and may even start laying aside money for the boy's future at that time.

The traditional family scenario has been quite different for females. College has often been viewed as a way for a girl to find a husband, as a diversion before entering into marriage, or as something she could do to prepare herself in case her husband should die or be unable to support her for some reason. When parents put away money for their daughters, it was usually for an elaborate wedding or a trust fund to take care of her in the event they died before she found a man. Even today, many women still work at menial jobs while putting their husbands through college since the perception is that it's more important for him to be educated because he has a better chance of making a good salary. It's not unusual for these women to subsequently be "dumped" by the educated husband when he finds that he has "grown" and she has not; he may conclude that they no longer have anything in common.

In order to move beyond the long-held notions that women can afford to neglect their education and training, women must insist that they (as well as their female offspring) be given the opportunity for that education and training, which will translate into financial independence. Even for those families with limited resources, loans and scholarships are available. However, we must be realistic: We can work, and we must work, to better ourselves, but even then we usually will have to work harder than a man to secure and maintain a job that is comparable to his. Some rather startling United Nations statistics were reported in 1992 by the Associated Press:

> Women in Sweden have 96 percent of the options that would allow them to lead as good a life as men, while women in Kenya have only a 58 percent chance. Other

countries listed are Finland, 94; France, 92; Paraguay, 88; UNITED STATES, 86; Canada, 85; Britain, 85; Italy and Portugal, 83; Japan, 77; Ireland, 74; Korea, 65.

Although collective attitudes often change at a snail's pace, and better opportunities take time to come to fruition, we can choose to enthusiastically push for those changes in every way that is available to us. For example, let's save our money to help our daughters go into business. Or, instead of paying for an expensive wedding ceremony, let's give them a down payment on real estate, or some other investment. Couples could share wedding expenses and cut down on the elaborate nature of the affair, if need be. Women need to think about their financial security just as early as men do. It's a mistake to wait to invest, buy real estate, and plan for a comfortable retirement. It's foolhardy to wait for someone else to take care of us. We must take responsibility for ourselves— and start to do so at an early age, as most boys are taught to do. A wise person once said that in order to be free, a person needs to stop collaborating with the captor. Women have been and still are captives of economic disadvantage. We must stop feeding this disadvantage and, instead, strive to effect positive change for ourselves and for one another.

One very effective method of working toward this change is through the act of mentoring. A mentor advises and encourages someone younger or someone in a less powerful position to attain her goals and to realize her full potential. Men have been functioning in this role for years, and we can be a part of this process, too. Successful, confident women can derive a considerable amount of satisfaction by helping women "on the way up" set realistic goals, plan a strategy for achieving them, and eventually seeing them enjoy financial independence.

For example, as part of a church program, a woman from Quincy, Massachusetts, invited a mother and daughter for dinner who had lived for many years in one homeless shelter after another. In 1990, she asked them to move in with her so that the two could get their lives together, and they've done just that. In the fall of 1994, the 17-year-old daughter entered Harvard University with a full scholarship!

It's Never Too Late to Learn and Progress

You may be reading this book at a time in your life when you're thinking: "It's too late for me!" Well, we don't believe that it's ever too late to explore creative alternatives, and there are more options than you know about at this moment! We would like to tell you about a very productive first step you might take, one that can lead to countless other opportunities. It doesn't matter if you're currently at the very lowest end of the economic ladder or even if you're on welfare—exploring this option can change your life for the better!

The fact is that most people live at least within commuting distance of a college or university. If, for whatever reason, you never graduated from high school, many colleges and universities offer programs designed to help students pass a high school equivalency exam and obtain a General Equivalency Diploma (GED). These programs also test students for aptitude and interest in various areas. Most schools will help women apply for loans and scholarships and even arrange for child care if necessary.

North Idaho College in Coeur d'Alene, Idaho, is an example of a school with a well-run program of this type, so we discussed the nature of their approach with director Carol Hauck and her assistant Sarah Hampton. They explained that similar programs started in the '70s were called Displaced Homemaker programs, but they have been updated to include women of all ages and circumstances. The North Idaho program, called The Center for New Directions, has a teen parenting program but also serves women who are well into their seventies. The classes at the Center are not conventional college classes, but are designed to give women hope by teaching them specific skills and providing information that encourages them to move beyond their fears and insecurities. Some of the women at the Center study for and pass the GED test; others need information about financial aid so they can enroll in college. There are also some who decide to concentrate on technical training instead of working towards a college degree. This type of instruction helps women break into nontraditional careers such as carpentry, drafting, and welding, which often pay generous salaries.

The entry class features components dealing with confidence-building and self-esteem, and goal-setting skills. It also guides women to job training and financial aid programs and gives them an overall view of the employment picture in the area. Another class, Enhancing Workplace Skills, helps students upgrade math, English, spelling, and mechanical reasoning abilities. There is also a free computer literacy program. In essence, this program is designed to help women get into college or into the workplace. Other classes offered are Parenting, Assertiveness, How to Get Out of Debt, and How to Eliminate Self-Defeating Behaviors—with personal counseling thrown in. There really is help out there! It's just a matter of seeking it out and being willing to ask for assistance.

One of the frustrations that some of the directors of these programs face is that so many otherwise intelligent women go through life with blinders on, they have done nothing to prepare themselves for taking care of themselves. Too many women assume that they don't count; they minimize the value of their natural abilities and don't believe they can handle change. However, just the fact that a woman is enrolled in a program such as the one described above shows that she has taken some initiative toward making a better life for herself.

The same is true for the readers of this book—you are looking for answers. That's the first step. We (the authors) both needed to extend ourselves well beyond easy and customary methods to obtain our educations, and we want to assure you that, with effort, you can achieve an education and the perks that go with it, too.

When her three children were still very young, Julie started to wonder what would happen if her husband lost his job. Although she had graduated from high school and had worked briefly for Michigan Bell as an operator, she felt ill-equipped to go out into the workplace. Her immediate solution was to sign up for correspondence courses in Business English. Eventually, she took the Newspaper Institute of American Writing class offered by correspondence and also a court reporting class from LaSalle Correspondence School. By preparing herself in this fashion, when her marriage ended, Julie was able to secure a secretarial job. She gradually started taking some college classes, and becoming more and more confident, she went on to obtain a bachelor's and a master's degree (with the help of loans and scholarships) and taught English at Ferris State University in Michigan. She had spanned a lengthy psychological distance between being a scared housewife with three small children and a lack of self-esteem to eventually teaching at the college level. In the course of teaching a Women's Studies class, she was able to utilize much of her own experience when helping other women to gain perspective and to claim their own power.

Ione's father died when she was 16, and her mother had only a fourth-grade education and worked at menial jobs, so there was no money for college. After high school, Ione went to work as a secretary for Mutual of Omaha and paid room and board to her mother. Ione hated her job and yearned to start college. Without Ione's knowledge, her mother saved the room-and-board money and offered it to Ione so she could enroll in school; it paid for one semester. Fortunately, Ione was able to get a secretarial job in the Dean of Students' office, supplementing that with baby-sitting jobs. She managed to get in two years of school before she married. She and her husband Ace worked very hard on a small Iowa farm and became the parents of a son. They looked into the ways in which Ione could survive and bring up their son if something happened to him.

Discovering that adequate insurance policies were beyond their financial reach, they came to the conclusion that the cheapest insurance would be for Ione to go back and finish her degree so that she could become a teacher. By attending school part time, she could still do her work on the farm and spend time with her child. Although paying tuition was often a challenge, Ione managed to finish the remaining two years toward her bachelor's degree in three-and-a-half years. After she started teaching and was bringing in a good income, her husband decided he'd like to become a minister. With Ione's blessings, he worked part time and went to school while Ione served as the primary support for the family. Some years later, Ione obtained her master's degree and went on to become very successful in the educational field.

We both strongly believe that the first and most important step a woman can take as she works toward self-sufficiency is to overcome any fear of getting out into the world to see what is available. Once a woman accomplishes this critical task, she will find that each subsequent step is much easier to take.

Erin—Shock and Recovery

Newspapers across the country periodically publish articles that chronicle women's issues and challenges. The story of a woman named Erin appeared in *The Spokesman-Review* in Spokane,

Washington, and we include it here because it perfectly illustrates that no matter how impossible circumstances may seem, it is indeed NEVER TOO LATE!

One week before Christmas in 1988, Erin was baking Christmas cookies with her two sons, ages two and four. She felt that everything was going as it should in her world, and she was grateful. This situation changed dramatically when her husband of 12 years came home and informed her that he had found someone else. He left home shortly thereafter, and Erin found herself stranded, with no skills, no money, and two children to raise. Erin had married at 18, and had always trusted her husband's words: "I'll always take care of you, baby." What follows is the rest of Erin's story, as she told it herself:

> After he walked out, I sat on the couch holding my babies and sobbing. The pain was nauseating. How would I live? How would I cope? I applied for public assistance. I stood in the line feeling humiliation and shame. I thought: "I wasn't raised for this." The children in line look dirty. Their mothers looked downtrodden. The people in charge were not friendly. Though my self-esteem was nonexistent at that point, I felt determined to not be on welfare forever.
>
> Then I heard about PROJECT SELF-HELP at Spokane Falls Community College. The three-month program helped me retrieve some of my self-esteem and helped me realize that to get off public assistance, I needed education. I attended Spokane Falls Community College for six quarters, then enrolled at Gonzaga University.
>
> Grants and loans paid my tuition. The children and I lived on $428 a month, plus $165 in food stamps. My ex-husband did not pay child support, although the courts ordered him to. I soon realized there were resources in the community for women like me, but I

had to energetically pursue them. I got involved in community activities and women's organizations, one of which gave me a $700 scholarship.

I even applied to Leadership Spokane, a program that prepares people to assume leadership roles in the community. Although I was rejected the first year, I was accepted the next. The program gave me a 75% scholarship, and a group of professional women raised the rest of the $1,200 tuition in one week.

In 1991, I graduated from Gonzaga with a 3.4 grade point average. I majored in communications and thought once I had the diploma, getting a job would be fairly easy. It wasn't. I filled out at least 100 job applications. One day I got a call from ARC, an organization that helps developmentally disabled people. I looked at the job description and said: "I can do it!" The woman who interviewed me later said that's why she gave me the job. I am coordinator of parent support and community outreach.

I am 35 years old and have 10,000 times more self-confidence than I did the day my husband walked out the door. I have self-esteem to share. The experience has given me much more compassion for women who struggle to make ends meet while raising small children.

I have some words of encouragement for women who might be in the same situation I was in a few years ago. Resources are out there, but you can't use them if you are going to sit there like a plant. Enroll in school. But don't depend just on the degree. Get involved in the community. Don't be afraid to walk through that door. If you don't step in, you won't know what's behind it.

There's an old riddle: "How do you eat an elephant?" The answer? "One bite at a time!" And once you've eaten one elephant, you're ready to try another one, only bigger.

(Courtesy *Spokesman-Review,* Spokane, WA)

Moving Beyond Basic Survival

Once a woman is making enough money to survive, what then? How can she move beyond basic survival? First of all, let's explore how a young woman might start out on this path. We share this information while acknowledging that when we were younger and could have applied these strategies, we didn't always know enough to do it. Please learn from our mistakes. We also realize that many of you readers are not young women (chronologically, that is), and the earlier a woman begins to make wise choices, the better, but it is never too late to begin putting viable money-making and money-managing strategies into effect.

Initially, a woman needs to realize how important it is to educate herself so she can be self-supporting, no matter what. Even if one is entering into a seemingly happy and secure marriage, as Erin seemed to be, it is important to become educated in some area that would allow for self-support if the necessity arises. Many women are choosing to be involved in a career from the start, while others have the priority of staying home with their children. Whatever the choice, a woman must be aware that the unexpected does occur, and that it's important to be prepared!

Buying a house is usually a good investment because it appreciates over time, can serve as an excellent tax deduction, and the equity in the home can be used to finance other necessities over the years. As we discussed in Chapter Two, a woman can ease the financial burden of home ownership by getting roommates, buying a duplex, or combining resources with other like-minded people. It is not uncommon for single mothers to buy a house together and enjoy the benefits of a shared lifestyle (remember the TV program of the 1980s, *Kate and Allie*?).

It is also essential to make a firm commitment to begin saving, no matter how small the amount. By taking at least a few dollars a month right off the top of your income, you invest in yourself and your future. Once a small nest egg is accrued, there are many expert financial planners that can advise those who do not feel secure or creative enough to invest on their own. Until a woman takes responsibility for herself, her lot in life will always be on a lower level than a man's. Marriages are enhanced when two people take responsibility for their mutual good and share life because they want to be together, not because one is too dependent for either to feel free. As for those women who don't marry, if they make wise financial choices, they will then have the means to build a life of their own choosing instead of one dictated solely by their financial status.

Bag Ladies of the World

Not too long ago, we spoke with the "founding mothers" of a group of women in Oregon who are creatively preparing for their later years. Unnerved by the grim statistics that predict that many women will end up alone, impoverished, and unable to care for themselves, these women have banded together to make sure that those statistics won't apply to them. They call themselves "The Bag Ladies of the World," but they point out that they don't intend to demean bag ladies. "Our name is our tongue-in-cheek contradiction of that possibility for us," they explain.

The idea was conceived when two friends, Ellen Weaver and Martha Snyder, realized that statistically they were then in their peak earning years. Concerned about their future, they joked about becoming bag ladies together. Suddenly they realized that they could begin right then and there to work toward a different outcome. Ellen organized a potluck dinner and invited their other women friends to explore the possibility of setting up a long-term support group. The idea struck a responsive chord, and the group eventually grew so large that offshoot groups sprang up, using the same model.

Now, each group has a bank account fueled by dues and fundraisers. In the future, they plan to purchase houses together, or perhaps duplexes or triplexes; the final arrangements are open-ended. What they do know is that they will be there for each other. The women range in age from 27 to 69, and the groups include both single and married women. The financial status of the women varies; some are professionals making a high salary while others are artists and homemakers with very little income. The thing they have in common is the desire to form kinship groups and develop long-term relationships and financial plans so they won't be alone or impoverished in their senior years.

The groups in Eugene, Florence, and Roseburg have monthly potlucks and semiannual retreats, they cook meals and prune trees together, and they make plans for a joint financial future. The eight groups of women who began meeting in 1985 have become a network of women committed to "graying" together. Their words of wisdom for other women who want to form similar groups: "Begin with women who already have history. Ellen and Martha have been friends for 20 years. As new people come into a group (ideally no more than 12), know that history can't be made overnight. Be patient, be focused on building trust and intimacy." The mother group has made a cassette tape that provides details and further advice. [2]

How Much Is Enough?

"He who knows he has enough is rich." — 3rd century B.C., Taoism

"He who dies with the most toys wins."— 20th century American

---

[2] Send $8.00, which includes postage, to Bag Ladies of the World, 3530 High Street, Eugene, OR 97405.

Obviously, the answer to the question of how much is enough will differ with each woman and her priorities. However, an increasing number of people in America are beginning to wonder if just accumulating "things" is all that satisfying. More and more women and men are seeking out the real priorities in their lives and making some changes, rejecting the consume-at-all-costs mentality and getting back to basics, simplifying their lives. In the process, they are finding that it is possible to live comfortably on much less than they previously thought they could.

Sometimes it takes a while to catch on that overspending can be just as addictive as overeating or drinking excessively. If we are honest with ourselves, most of us would have to admit that, at one time or another, we've spent money just to make ourselves feel better. Many women, including ourselves, have overspent for that very reason, and also just to alleviate boredom at times. Currently, over 90 percent of American teenage girls report store-hopping as their favorite activity. Ironically, in 1987 the number of shopping centers surpassed the number of high schools in our country!

For the past three decades, Americans have been consuming more and more, but at the same time, they feel that their quality of life is declining. Per capita consumption in the U.S. has risen 45 percent in the last 20 years, but the decrease in the quality of life in the U.S. since 1970, as measured by the Index of Social Health, has been 51 percent. Perhaps the most startling statistic of all is that the average European produces less than half the waste that the average American does. While Americans make up only 5 percent of the world's population, we use 30 percent of the world's resources.

For the planet to comfortably support everyone on it without endangering the world's resources, we would have to live as the Europeans do. They have modest but comfortable homes, ready access to public transit, and limit their auto use. [3]

---

[3] Statistics from *ALL-CONSUMING PASSION, Waking Up From the American Dream*. Booklet is $1 and may be ordered from Q.T.S., P. O. Box 15352, Seattle WA 98115.

It's clear that the mere act of consuming more is not going to make our quality of life any better. This is a lesson we all need to learn, not just for our own sake but for the sake of the planet as well. Most of us have grown up believing that if we wanted to live a happy and fulfilled life, that if we wanted to be free to travel or do other things that are important to us, we'd need to find a way to make lots of money. Certainly, there is nothing wrong in being affluent, but even more important than making money is learning to use money creatively and wisely and truly improving the quality of our lives, not just working harder and harder to accumulate more things. We need to remember that it is possible to live on income from wise investments, which would allow us freedom to pursue whatever creative or philanthropic activity we desire.

What are some practical things that we can do to become more responsible and creative with our money? Toward this end, we offer some strategies that can help make it easier to live a more creative, fulfilling, and comfortable life on a modest budget. They've been tested and tried by us and by other women as well—they really work!

Define Material Goals

A wise woman once said: "You can have anything, but you can't have everything." Too often we're vague about just what it is we do want. We often clump our desires together into a collection of "I'll do that or have that some day when my ship comes in." It is often worthwhile to ask ourselves such questions as, "What is the one place in the world I want to visit before I die? What am I willing to give up in order to go there? What material possessions are important to me, and what am I willing to forego?" It's also helpful to make a list of things you'd like to have and do in the next year, five years, and ten years and number them in order of importance. Suppose your number-one material goal is to save enough for a down payment on a home, and your number-three material goal is to possess a ruby ring. Ruby rings have just gone on sale, and you are tempted to go ahead and buy one. It might be easier to resist that temptation if you have made a priority list and have committed to the order of that list. All too often lesser desires distract us from our main goals.

Set Priorities and Goals Beyond Material Ones

We know that setting lofty goals is difficult to do when basic survival is at stake. However, the Biblical statement that "man does not live by bread alone" is true. It's important for each one of us to answer questions such as: "What are the things I'd like to accomplish in this life? How do I want to spend my time? Is it more important for me to have lots of money in the bank, or would I rather have time to do what I want?" We've found that at different ages and stages in our lives, the answers may vary.

Julie counseled several students each term when she was teaching. One aspect of that counseling involved helping students define their career goals. From her own experience, she realized that studying something just because it looked like it would lead to solid employment after graduation was not a good enough reason to do it. Oftentimes, by the time the student graduated, the job market had shifted so that the student's course of study did not necessarily guarantee anything. For that reason, she always urged students to pursue those interests that delighted and stimulated them—what seemed to come naturally to them. She suggested that they think of something that they would still do even if they were independently wealthy!

Since most people are going to have to work at least a good part of their lives to earn a living, why not do something that is truly satisfying? Incredibly, the usual outcome is that when a person really loves what she is doing, she does it better and is apt to be adequately reimbursed for doing it! Even if there seems to be vigorous competition in a field, those who are enthusiastic and dive into that area for the love of it are the ones who will get and keep the work.

Strategies for Living Well on Less Money

◆ CONSIDER COOPERATIVE INVESTMENTS AND SHARED LIVING

As we've stated repeatedly in this book, it's possible to enjoy a much higher standard of living by sharing resources with others.

◆ SHOP AT FOOD COOPERATIVES AND DISCOUNT GROCERY STORES

Even after we buy a membership, the savings are great! Also, many dollars can be saved by CLIPPING COUPONS!

◆ PUT TOGETHER A SHOPPING DIRECTORY FOR WOMEN

Organize friends, relatives, and groups who can help you put together a directory of merchants and service providers that deal with women fairly and courteously. As a result, you will end up with a list of the most reputable auto dealers, service stations and garages, repair shops of all kinds, furniture stores, appliance dealers; home repairmen such as painters, carpenters, plumbers, roofers, and any others you can think of! Let the merchants know you're compiling a directory. Perhaps they will offer discounts to women, and they might even contribute to the labor and cost of printing the directory. We needn't allow ourselves to be taken advantage of!

◆ DRIVE USED CARS

Take time to research the most reliable makes and models, then shop around and don't be in a hurry to buy. If you are not mechanically savvy, ask a friend who is in the know to accompany you when you check out cars. If you know someone who works as a mechanic for a dealership, ask him or her to be on the lookout for a good used car that comes in as a trade-in. Cars depreciate thousands of dollars the moment they are driven off the lot. The authors drive older cars (not junkers, yet still good-looking, safe, and serviceable) to travel about our immediate area. When we take a long cross-county trip, we rent a newer car with unlimited mileage as part of the package. This strategy is less costly in the long run.

◆ BUY USED FURNITURE, CLOTHING, AND OTHER ITEMS

A friend of ours keeps her two grandsons very nicely clothed by shopping at garage sales. Also, there are many fine used clothing stores specifically for children and for women. Because children grow so quickly, they usually don't wear out their clothes. When you buy anything used, if you will take the time to check out the condition and quality of the item, you'll find many good bargains out there!

◆ BE CAREFUL WITH CREDIT CARDS

If you know you're an impulse spender, leave your credit cards at home. If you don't know how or when you can pay for what you charge on your card, don't do it! It's especially difficult to pay for dead horses like restaurant meals, gas, vacations. Paying as you go is the best way to avoid getting in over your head. When you must use your credit card, deduct the amount from your check register at the time of the purchase. This will not only give you an accurate picture of your financial position, but when you receive your credit card bill, you will just be able to write out a check, knowing that, in a way, you've already "paid" for the item.

In today's society, a credit card is a must if you want to rent a car or reserve a hotel room or secure many other types of services. However, credit cards come with very different terms. Shop around and find one with no annual fee and the lowest interest rate. It's best to pay off any balance each month before you have to pay any finance charges, but if at times you need to carry over your balance, naturally you will want to pay the lowest possible interest.

◆ DISCOUNT STORES, SALES, COMPARISON
SHOPPING

The same item can sell for a wide range of prices. Why pay the high one? It definitely pays to research the market. You can often make phone calls to weed out the establishments that are too expensive.

◆ TAKE CARE OF YOUR POSSESSIONS

Change the oil in your car on time, and adhere to the maintenance schedule in your owner's manual. When one of your appliances needs to be repaired, take care of the problem immediately. Keep all of your possessions clean and maintained. It pays in the long run.

◆ TAKE CARE OF YOURSELF

Good health habits such as eating and exercising properly, not smoking, not abusing alcohol or drugs, and maintaining a positive attitude can ultimately save thousands in doctor bills! (Insurance rates will be less costly, too.)

◆ VISIT YOUR LOCAL LIBRARY

There's a wealth of fascinating reading out there that doesn't cost anything! Most novels and magazines are read once and then either never opened again or discarded. By frequenting your local library, you can read all the fiction and periodicals you wish without having to make a single purchase. Most libraries buy the current bestsellers and popular magazines. You may have to place your name on a list and wait awhile, but even current bestsellers are available at no cost. Borrowing books from the library is also a great way to find out which books you'd like to buy for your home library. It's like getting a no-commitment, free trial period with every book!

◆ ATTEND BARGAIN MATINEES OR RENT FILMS ON VIDEO

Most cinemas feature bargain matinees before 6:00 p.m. on weekdays and during certain hours on weekends and holidays. Senior citizen rates are usually the same at any time of the day or week. Or, you can wait until films go to video and watch them at your convenience at home!

◆ IF YOU ARE A SENIOR CITIZEN, TAKE ADVANTAGE OF MANY OTHER DISCOUNTS OFFERED BY:

Airlines (discount booklets for those over 62), Amtrak, restaurants with senior menus, national parks, museums, and amusement parks offering discounts; and most banks (which may offer free checks and checking accounts and other discount services). Remember: Qualifying ages vary, so it pays to shop around!

◆ SEEK OTHER MONEY-SAVING STRATEGIES

Brainstorm with friends. Make it a creative and fun challenge to live better on less!

◆ BE GENEROUS

Don't be afraid to be generous. Give money where you feel it counts the most. Volunteer your services. Make a positive difference, and you will be richer for it! Give your best to the Universe, and the Universe will give its best back to you!

❖ SUMMING UP ❖

Statistics show us that it is still difficult for women to be on an equal financial footing with men. However, there are specific strategies we can employ to make ourselves exceptions to those statistics. We can begin right now, in whatever situation we find ourselves, to make positive changes that will financially empower us. We do have the wherewithal to gain financial independence; we can have abundance and still be responsible caretakers of our planet. Let us clarify our priorities, set our goals, and then do whatever we can to attain them!

Action Steps

◆ Invite a group of women friends over for a potluck dinner to explore how you might improve your financial situations and how you might cooperate with each other. Use the ideas in this chapter as a basis for the discussion. You might decide to form a financial support group that would meet on a regular basis.

◆ Education can be a crucial key to improving your financial situation. If you need more education, go to the nearest community college and check out what's available for women. If you need financial help, check with the Financial Aid office. Even if it might be awhile before you can begin, explore the opportunities NOW! Visualize yourself being a success!

◆ Begin the habit of saving, no matter how little you have to start with. Even if it's only a dollar a week, start to save NOW!

◆ Make a list of your goals and priorities, including the non-material ones. What do you want to see happen in your life in the next year, the next two years, the next five years? Make separate lists for each time period, and prioritize the goals on each one.

◆ Start being a smart consumer by utilizing some of the money-saving strategies listed in this chapter. Keep track of how much you save.

◆ Increase your awareness of your spending even more by keeping track of ALL your expenditures for a month! A small notebook that can be carried in your purse is essential. At the end of the month, review your notes and separate those items that are essential from those items that are nonessential. Also mark those products or services that are nonessential, but which you are not willing to give up (such as cable TV or home delivery of your newspaper). Assess where you can trim your budget.

◆ If you want to take these suggestions even further, the book, *Your Money or Your Life,* by Dominquez and Robin, provides an excellent step-by-step strategy for defining priorities and getting your financial life together, no matter what your starting point.

◆ Mentoring: If you are already financially secure, help at least one other woman in whatever ways are appropriate (low-interest loan, scholarship, help with child care or housing, as well as your friendship and encouragement).

◆ Affirm often: *"I take responsibility for my financial well-being. I set financial goals and work toward them. I give my best to the world, and the world gives its best back to me. I am abundantly provided for, and I am grateful!"*

CHAPTER   FIVE

MAKING HEALTHY CHOICES,
MAKING HEALING CHOICES

"The biochemistry of the body is a product of awareness."

—Deepak Chopra, M.D.

It is frightening to think that we may reach a point in our lives when we lose control. While we can seemingly lose control over our lives in many ways, such as through lack of finances, loss of relationships, or job loss, none seems quite as paralyzing as the loss of our physical health. As long as we remain healthy, we can manage to care for our physical needs in some manner. At the very least, we can usually find someone willing to help us or point the way to available resources. But for those of us who have prided ourselves on our independence, loss of physical health seems fundamentally terrifying.

One woman we spoke to pointed out that she couldn't even find someone to take her to the dentist to have her wisdom teeth pulled. So what would the prospects be if she had a debilitating illness that might go on for months or years? These are all real concerns being faced every day by the woman who is alone. In some cases, there might be children or other family members willing to help out, but just as often, those extended family members live in other areas of the country or world and have their own busy lives and demanding careers. How would we cope with a short- or long-term health problem? This question demands some thoughtful exploration, and it's important that we, as women alone, share our insights and creative solutions.

We have already discussed at length the physical and emotional support systems that some people have set up for themselves through community, whether in the form of shared housing, or separate housing but shared lives. These support systems are crucial for most women alone. It has been well documented that single people are ill more frequently and tend to die at an earlier age than their married or "companioned" counterparts. So, setting up an emotional and, if possible, a physical support system, seems like a wonderful place to begin.

Also, from a practical level, if you have not appointed someone you trust to make health decisions for you in the event you are unable to make them for yourself, this would be a good time to think about doing so. The four of us at the Holo Center have legal documents naming one another to make such decisions for us in the event of a sudden illness or accident. Even though we are women with adult children, we have to consider that our sons and daughters all live outside of our geographical location and are often busy and difficult to reach. Besides, a sudden illness or accident could require an on-the-spot decision, and who is better qualified to make those decisions than the people with whom we share the intimacy of our day-to-day process? Since we all discuss these issues often, we feel that we know more than any of our children do about our specific wants and needs. However, we can also count on one another to be very sensitive to what each of our children feels and to listen to what they would have to say about any particular matter.

We must also be willing to take responsibility for maintaining our own health by eating right, exercising, and achieving a sound balance between productivity and leisure. We need to seek out a physician who is willing to cooperate with our efforts to lead a healthful lifestyle. Let's not simply turn over our bodies and minds to someone else blindly. We need to help our doctor(s) make the decisions about our physical and emotional well-being and insist on being informed of all the alternatives in cases of illness.

Eating Right

Take the responsibility for choosing foods that are healthful. Most research seems to indicate that our diet ought to consist primarily of fruits, vegetables, and whole grains. It also tells us to reduce much of our fat intake and to limit foods with sugar. These recommendations will also help us lose weight, if necessary, and will supply our bodies with the best possible nutrients to maintain optimum health. Eliminating all but the smallest amount of animal protein in our diet saves more than enough money to allow us to enjoy wonderful fresh fruits and vegetables, even when they are out of season.

One middle-aged woman we interviewed asked herself, What is healthy for me? She researched the question, and on the basis of the information she gleaned, decided to become a strict live-foods vegetarian. She reported to us that she has significantly improved her health. She now eats slowly and meditatively, understanding the vital link between the body, mind, and spirit. Smooth skin, a supple, agile body, and a timeless look all defied us to come within 20 years of her actual age. Only when she revealed all that she had done in her lifetime and the dates that these events had occurred, were we able to discern this woman's age. We were truly impressed.

This woman also mentioned that most people she knows are into cooking, eating, and watching another video, with six more stacked up behind it. She, on the other hand, likes to use her whole brain to both think and intuit. She revels in meaningful work and days filled with sun, rest, and solitude. She believes that when she began to adhere to a cleansing diet, all her hidden addictions started to fall by the wayside.

Many health-conscious women take food supplements in the form of vitamins and herbs as part of their health regimen. There is mounting medical evidence to support the argument that additional quantities of certain vitamins can be helpful in preventing many diseases. You may wish to look at your own risk factors for various illnesses and put yourself on a moderate supplemental program. Such an approach, however, must never be used as a substitute for eating healthfully. The most nutritionally sound foods are still derived from the fresh fruits, vegetables, and whole grains that we eat on a daily basis.

The Benefits of Exercise

As a nation, we have had a tendency to become a nation of "watchers," and in the process, we've forgotten how to participate. It is much easier to watch a ball game on TV than to go outside and play one (or to even attend one at a ballpark). We need to become a nation of "movers" again. During the earlier years of our nation's history, the bulk of labor performed was physical. In our modern, computer-driven society, that is no longer the case, so we must consciously make time to exercise more—whether this simply involves parking the car in the last parking spot in the mall and walking across the entire lot—or embarking on a rigid exercise program. New studies prove that we do not have to do intense work such as running five miles, climbing a mountain, bicycling across the city, and so on, to reap optimum benefits from exercise. Just thirty minutes, three times a week, of light aerobic exercise can make you healthier and more fit.

There are many forms of exercise from which a woman can choose. Walking is inexpensive and very beneficial. Swimming, water aerobics, tennis, and cross-country skiing are also some of the best all-around exercises that you can do. There are outlets for exercise available to all ages, all sizes, all personal preferences, and many are free or inexpensive. There are very few reasons or excuses we can give for not participating in some form of physical activity. However, if you are older, or are uncertain about which form of exercise would be most appropriate for you, you would be wise to check with your doctor.

At the Holo Community, we chop wood, haul it, and stack it daily during the months that we have fires. It affords several minutes of vigorous activity. We built our swimming pool so that we could swim year-round and for as many years as we can get in and out of the pool. Whatever your budget and interest allows, pursue some form of exercise. You'll feel better and live longer!

Balancing Productivity and Leisure

Living a balanced lifestyle—that is, one which encompasses equal doses of work that we enjoy and leisure activities that provide relaxation and pleasure—is essential to good health. As far as our professional life is concerned, it needs to be stimulating and satisfying on many levels. For example, Ione worked in the field of education for 12 years and says that she can't remember a time when she didn't enjoy her job and look forward to going to work in the morning. If going to a job feels like daily drudgery, perhaps it's time to carefully examine what it is we're doing. We give ourselves a wonderful gift if we can figure out what we love to do, then find a way to make a living doing it. (An excellent book that addresses these issues is *When 9 to 5 Isn't Enough,* by Marcia Perkins-Reed.)

Nevertheless, once we've left the job behind, no matter how enjoyable it is, we need to concentrate on finding a balance between active and inactive pursuits that allow a shift into a totally different realm. We need to create something, have fun, or withdraw into quiet solitude; we simply need to take a break from the everyday work routine. All-around good health requires balance in both our inner and outer lives, equal amounts of work and play.

We all need outlets for expressing ourselves creatively. Something vital within us is blocked if we are not involved in some form of creative expression at some point in our lives. Perhaps we need to write a book, draw or paint a picture, or maybe there is a song within us that needs to be sung, a floral arrangement to be made, a cake to be decorated, a new gourmet dish to cook, beads to be formed into jewelry, a flower garden to plant, a garment to be sewn, a letter to be written, a journal to record, a pot to be turned on the potter's wheel, a dream to unravel, or any other pursuit that flows from within. Women were born to create, so if we allow our creative flow to be dammed up by responsibilities, it is detrimental to our bodies, our minds, and our spirits. When creativity flows, the other areas of our lives flow more easily and efficiently as well.

Self-Healing

There are numerous self-healing techniques that we can utilize for maximum health benefits. While traditional medicine and prescription drugs are often of great value, they have also tended to be overused in many instances. Recently, many of those in the medical community have written books that have promoted more cooperation between patient and physician in maintaining good health and which have advocated alternative therapies in place of pills, injections, and surgeries. In the book, *Reversing Heart Disease,* Dr. Dean Ornish promotes a nutritious diet, regular exercise, and meditation. Mutual of Omaha, one of the country's largest health insurers, encourages policy holders with heart disease to take wellness classes based on Dr. Ornish's research, and they are even willing to pay for them. We know that the only reason any insurer would pay for this program is because it works, thus saving the insurers considerable amounts of money that would otherwise be used to cover medical claims.

In addition to meditation, some self-help tools that help improve and maintain one's health include visualization, affirmations, dream 'work, and journaling. Research has shown that journaling (see Chapter One for more details) actually boosts our immune systems; furthermore, the benefits last for at least six weeks. It is also helpful to use dialoguing, a technique where we talk to the body to gain insights from it, to heal the maladies that afflict us. Dreams often symbolically reveal the state of our health, and the ancient Greeks had dream temples where people went to dream their healing, often with great success. There are many viable and helpful alternatives that can be explored by those with open minds, and books on these subjects are available in most bookstores.

Exploring the Body-Mind Connection

As our knowledge and understanding of the body-mind connection grows, many of us are looking honestly at our attitudes and the unhealed areas of our lives. A number of women are starting to work with their "inner child" and are exploring the process of re-parenting. Old wounds and negative past programming can be replaced with healthier ways of thinking and living, but we must understand that our thoughts and feelings have a direct influence upon our bodies.

A woman whom we counsel has spent more than half of her 33 years labeled as clinically emotionally disabled and has lived on Social Security benefits as a result of her inability to function. She has literally blossomed during the last few months as a result of intensive inner healing therapy and classes geared specifically to empower her to take charge of her own well-being. In the process, her physical health has also improved, and she recently informed us that she is in absolute awe of the power of the body-mind connection. She has been willing to really "dig in" and work on getting well, becoming a faithful observer of her thoughts and actions. Most importantly, she has taken action and really made an effort to apply every technique she's learned to her own life, and she has been willing to take increasing responsibility for how she thinks and how she handles situations. We could fill a separate book with stories of women who have experienced miraculous transformations, but instead, we will just fill a chapter with the stories of the three women described below.

Bobbie—A Powerful Choice

Bobbie was a good friend who had multiple sclerosis. She had been ill for several years and was wheelchair bound. Ione suggested one day during a visit that sometimes people with debilitating illnesses are trying to gain control over situations they feel powerless to change. She asked Bobbie to consider whether that concept held any truth for her. After thinking about it for a few minutes, Bobbie replied that it was possible because her husband had not always been faithful, and her illness kept him more confined during the evening hours.

Ione asked Bobbie, "Are you willing to be well even if it means losing your husband?" Bobbie sat silently for a long time, and then the tears started to trickle down her cheeks. "Losing him would be too high a price to pay," Bobbie finally answered, admitting that she would rather be incapacitated than lose her husband. Ione moved away and didn't hear from her for about two years, when she received a letter from Bobbie. She wrote about swimming every day and of a planned trip to Europe, adding a postscript: "In case you're wondering, I finally decided that no man is worth it!" Ironically, after Bobbie had dealt with her self-esteem and control issues and had improved her health, she and her husband patched up their differences, too.

Masil—The Power of Inner Healing

Our friend Masil used to suffer from nontropical sprue, an allergy to all forms of gluten, such as wheat, oats, barley, and rye. Medically, it's termed an incurable disease. She lived with this malady for 16 years, and it severely restricted her life. She had to read all labels carefully and carry food with her when she traveled because her diet was so limited. Even a small amount of gluten caused days of uncontrollable diarrhea that badly depleted her body. One month she lost 25 pounds.

When Masil came to Ione for counseling, Ione asked her how she had dealt with the tragic accident that had befallen her two sons 16 years earlier. Masil's boys, ages seven and ten, had found dynamite caps, and not realizing the danger, began to play with them. They exploded, killing the oldest boy, and blinding Dave, the younger son.

Since Masil was a registered nurse as well as a devoted mother, she kept busy caring for Dave, leaving his side only long enough to

attend her other son's funeral. In an attempt to save his eyesight, doctors instructed her not to allow Dave to cry, and there didn't seem to
be any time or space allowed for Masil to cry or grieve her own loss.
For six months, she just did what had to be done. By the time Dave
lost his sight and was enrolled in a school for the blind, she had sup-
pressed her feelings for so long that she was no longer able to cry.

Sixteen years later, while in therapy, Ione took Masil back in time
to deal with the accident and to complete the grieving process step
by step. After that task was accomplished, they agreed to try to facilitate the healing of Masil's sprue. They went to the mountains and
fasted and prayed, and then Ione placed her hands on Masil's
abdomen while they both visualized a perfect intestinal tract. They
could feel Masil's entire abdomen moving, and Masil had the strong
sense that she was healed. After they returned home, Masil ate a
hamburger bun and a doughnut, her first in many years, with no
adverse reaction.

That was in 1976, and she has never had a recurrence of that ail-
ment. She continues to eat anything she wants, whenever she
wants. One can only speculate why the illness took the form of an
allergy to wheat products, but it is fascinating to note that her boys'
accident took place in a wheat field!

Eunice—A Second Chance

Eunice, a childless widow in her late seventies, was living alone
when Ione and Masil used to visit with her. Time and again, she
stated that she wouldn't mind living in a nursing home if it became
necessary. Ione and Masil recognized that she was not merely
resigned to the possibility; she was actually looking forward to it.

Eventually, the time came when she was hospitalized with an
extended illness and then moved into a full-care facility. For a very
brief time she seemed content there, once even referring to it acci-

dentally as a hotel. However, before long, her visions of being in a hotel with room service were rudely interrupted by reality. She began to complain: She was only bathed once a week. Aides didn't always answer her call button. The meals were not as tasty as the ones she fixed for herself, and they weren't served hot enough. She grew more discontent with the passing weeks.

On one visit, Ione and Masil said to her, "Since your apartment has not been emptied yet, why not consider getting well and moving back home?" It hadn't occurred to Eunice that she could get well, but she accepted this new idea, determined to leave the nursing home. In a short time, she was indeed well enough to return to her own little apartment.

Eunice lived quite well on her own for several years. On the day she made her transition, she was on her way to a community luncheon at a local church. Ione's husband had taken his car to get her, and as he was telling her a funny story and escorting her up the steps, she collapsed and died right in the middle of her laughter. No doubt most of us would rather die while active and laughing than in a hospital or nursing home. Eunice's decision to get well and return to her home illustrates how the power of our minds, and how our beliefs and attitudes, can influence how we will live and how we will die. (The book, *The Power of the Mind to Heal,* by Drs. Joan and Miroslav Borysenko, illustrates these concepts beautifully.)

The Ultimate Goal

We firmly believe that everyone must find something greater than themselves to believe in. We would not try to impose any specific brand of religion on our readers, but a spiritual or cosmic overview seems essential for most of us in order to maintain a healthy body and mind. Our finite lives can lose their focus unless we can view our existence from a larger perspective.

Who am I? What is the meaning of life? What is my relationship to other human beings? Those are the questions that we all ultimately seek to answer. However, the answers do not lie outside ourselves, nor does the help we seek. We only need open our minds and hearts to the greater spiritual wisdom, the higher power that flows through our daily lives.

We are body, we are mind, and we are spirit. Indeed, the newest field of science, quantum physics, repeatedly submits that we are multidimensional beings capable of much more than our five senses would suggest. Gary Zukav provides a physicist's view of our greater potential in his book, *Seat of the Soul.* We need to consider that potential and all three aspects of ourselves when we think in terms of our life and, specifically, our health.

Our goal as evolving human beings who also happen to be women alone is the integration of body, mind, and spirit. As this integration takes place, we will transcend "me" and "mine" and begin to reflect wholeness and love, increasing the likelihood that we will live out our lives in good health. And when the moment of physical death arrives, we will have taken care of our unfinished business and balanced our inner and outer journeys, and we will be able to exit the body, freely, easily, and gently.

❖ SUMMING UP ❖

In spite of our best efforts to prepare for the future and to provide for our health needs, there is always the possibility that an accident or illness of some type will disrupt our lives. In the event that the unexpected occurs, we need to move beyond blaming ourselves and embrace the realization that everything is a facet of our existence from which we can find meaning and purpose. However, there are several things we can do that give us a far greater chance for living a long and healthy life. We can all take greater responsibility for working with the body/mind/spirit connection and for balancing our life by making certain there is time for work and play, time for interacting with others and for solitude, time for giving and receiving, and time for humor amidst the seriousness of life. We need to take daily responsibility for our thoughts and attitudes and for our own well-being. We need to connect with the Divine, in whatever form we know that to be, and then rest in infinite good.

Action Steps

♦ Think about a person in your life whom you would trust to make health-care decisions for you if you should become unable to make them for yourself. Ask this person if he or she is willing to undertake this responsibility and, if so, take the necessary legal steps to ensure that your wishes will be honored.

♦ Be sure you have a living will drawn up that specifies your intent. Your local hospital can advise you on this matter.

♦ Take responsibility for maintaining good physical health:

    a. include adequate amounts of fruits, vegetables, and grains in your daily diet

    b. consider what vitamins and supplements might be helpful in light of your personal history

    c. make sure you exercise on a daily basis

♦ Take good care of your mental health, as well:

    a. relax each day in silence or meditation

  b. pay attention to your thinking and speaking pat-
     terns, and work to improve those atttitudes that are
     unproductive

◆ Nurture your spiritual side:

  a. read something inspirational each day
  b. take time to connect with the Higher Power
  c. develop your intuition and listen to your inner voice

◆ Find time each day to be productive, and also make time for
  fun and laughter.

◆ Read Louise Hay's book, *You Can Heal Your Life*. Louise
  offers valuable information on body/mind connections and
  shows how to dissolve "both the fears and causations of diseases." Her message is: "If we are willing to do the mental
  work, almost anything can be healed."

◆ The best foundation for good health is a life that is joyous,
  satisfying, and meaningful. So, find ways to inject a spirit of
  adventure into your daily activities, and begin to build mutual emotional and physical support systems.

◆ Affirm the following every day: *"My body is made of the
  non-aging, non-deteriorating substance of God. I revel in its
  increasing vigor; I revel in its perfect health. I revel that
  every atom, every cell, every organ of my body vibrates with
  the divine life of God and, therefore, is perfect, even as God
  is perfect. I give praise for it, I give thanks for it; I bless it for
  being what it is—the outermost layer of my soul."* (This affirmation was given to Ione many decades ago by her spiritual
  teacher, Agnes Sanford.)

❖ ❖ ❖

CHAPTER SIX

PARENTING WITH CONFIDENCE

"There are only two lasting bequests we can hope to give our children. One of these is roots, the other wings."

— Hodding Carter, author and statesman

In the strictest sense of the word, a woman is not totally *alone* when she has children living with her. Yet, she is often alone with her responsibility, alone with her concerns about money, and alone with her own needs, hopes, and dreams. No matter what circumstances contributed to a woman's role as a single parent, it is rarely an easy position. Parenting is a considerable challenge these days for even the most stable of two-parent families, let alone for one headed by a single parent—especially one that may be experiencing the devastating trauma of a family torn apart by death or divorce.

However, even those unmarried women who have chosen to give birth to or adopt a child find that the demands are often more daunting than they could have imagined. What can lessen the burden, though, is the knowledge that there are resources out there that can make a positive difference. (We will delineate some of these later in the chapter.)

Now, it certainly is possible for one person to lovingly and effectively parent a child. True, this situation presents its own unique trials and difficulties, but many committed single parents *are* successfully dealing with this type of family arrangement. Even in two-parent families, sometimes one parent (most often the woman), takes on the majority of the actual parenting responsibilities. This predicament can occur as a result of a father who works long hours or has two jobs, is addicted to alcohol or drugs, has priorities other than his children, or is in one of the armed services and away from home for months at a time.

Ione, herself, was the primary caregiver to her children. Her husband worked long hours and two jobs for many years, eventually entering the ministry, which left him very little time to spend with his family. Julie was married to a pipeline superintendent who traveled to all parts of the country, wherever the job was, and when he was home, he still spent much time away from his family. She was, for all practical purposes, a single parent, even prior to her divorce. As we look around us, we can see that, for a variety of reasons, partnered women are often thrust into the role of the single parent.

In Ione's family of origin, her mother took on the majority of the parenting responsibilities because her father worked long hours; later he was injured and spent extended periods of time in a veterans' hospital. Ione could always feel the love that her parents felt for her, and she knew that they would do anything they could for her, but because her mother was a strict disciplinarian, and since the family had financial difficulties, Ione was made aware that she had to contribute in whatever way she could to the household. She feels that her early experiences helped her build the discipline that she would eventually need in her adult years, and also gave her the confidence to believe that she could always find a way to work through any problem. In Julie's adopted family, her mother was the responsible parent because Julie's father was lost in the throes of alcoholism. As a result of the family's precarious financial state, Julie worked, took care of her own needs, and contributed to the family during her high school years. Like Ione, she is certain that these early trials and tribulations helped her become a strong and self-reliant woman who could always count on herself to survive in any situation.

Women who are functioning as single parents need to remember one very important thing, even at times when the challenges seem overwhelming: If you are a loving and communicative parent (not necessarily a perfect parent) who lets your child or children know how much you care, your children have an excellent chance of growing up to be productive, happy, self-assured adults!

Avoid the Victim Trap

As we mentioned, a woman alone faces formidable challenges when placed in the position of having to raise her children by herself. If the father is not providing financial support (either in or out of marriage), or if there is inadequate insurance, a woman is subjected to extreme pressure on many levels. For many women alone, the financial challenge is THE primary concern, and for that reason, we've devoted an entire chapter to that subject.

Yet, in spite of the demands, there is one pitfall that women must avoid at all costs: the victim trap. Basically, as long as a woman feels and acts like a victim, she will remain one. The price she pays for allowing herself to fall into accepting this role is very high: A victim feels habitually helpless, hopeless, depressed, and immobile. The only way to stay out of that trap is to be aware that it exists and that she must use every ounce of courage, self-reliance, and intelligence to find a way out.

Julie was thrust into the single-parenting role only one year after her oldest son Richard had died. Only 29 years old at the time, she felt very inadequate to the task. It was a frightening and unhappy time in her life—a period when she made many mistakes; it took several years for her to completely erase her victim mentality. However, she found that by meeting each day's challenges as they came, she did manage to survive. She remembers one Christmas Day when the children were with their father. On Christmas Eve, Julie and the children had been together with her family, but on Christmas Day, she found herself alone. What to do? She realized that she had a choice. She could choose to feel depressed and miserable, or she could find a way to make the best of it. So, she decided to relax and read a good book. When it was time to eat, she made herself a sandwich from some sausage that was in the refrigerator. The experience turned out to be a very empowering one for her because at least for that day, she managed to break away from a despondent victim mode by choosing a more productive response to the situation.

What Do We Tell the Children?

It can be tempting to make oneself a victim and the "wronged one" because we want our children to be "on our side." This helps no one, least of all the children. No matter how despicable we feel the father of our children may be, it's not wise to bad-mouth him. Of course, tell the truth, even if the father is in jail, but try to separate his unacceptable behavior from the essential nature of the person, who has made a mistake he must pay for. If he has caused harm to his children or to you, or you sincerely believe he represents a future danger to you or your children, then your primary responsibility, naturally, is to maintain your family's safety. Just remember that his blood also runs through the veins of your children. Help them see the person he might have been under different circumstances so that they don't have to carry around a burden of guilt and shame for the rest of their lives.

Julie experienced the pain of being born out of wedlock to a 15-year-old who had been raped by her stepfather. The knowledge that her own "flesh and blood" could do something so horrible no doubt contributed to her long and difficult struggle to continually prove her worth, and reinforced her feelings that she would never be good enough. Fortunately, she learned how to differentiate reprehensible behavior from the basic goodness of each soul, and was then able to come to acceptable terms with her situation.

Sometimes, even when a former spouse has been a good parent and wants to continue a relationship with the children, the other parent will retaliate by making that involvement difficult. This is self-defeating for both parents and harmful to the child. It takes self-discipline and maturity to handle the presence of an ex-partner, but if it can be done in a positive way, both children and parents will eventually reap the rewards. Melinda Blau, author of the book, *Families Apart,* offers additional wisdom that can help divorced parents and their children. She discusses the need for a parent to take responsibility for self-healing and points out the danger of trying to make any child a surrogate spouse; the goal is to act in a mature fashion, no matter how difficult that may be.

As a result of Julie's own experience, she knew that it would be harmful to her children to criticize their father in front of them. Although he left her for another woman, which brought up her abandonment issues, and even though she didn't know how she was going to support herself and the children, she always tried to help her children see their father's positive qualities. She reminded them often that he loved them, while at the same time not concealing the fact that he had an alcohol problem. Eventually, with support and therapy, Julie managed to work through her negative emotions without subjecting her children to the frustration she was experiencing.

The ultimate test came years later when Julie's daughter Colleen married. The bride-to-be wanted her father to walk her down the aisle, her half-sisters to be bridesmaids, and since Julie was a minister, Colleen wanted her mother to perform the ceremony. This turn of events is exactly what eventually ensued, and in spite of Julie's conflicted inner feelings, and probably those of the others as well, everything went very smoothly and amicably. Julie has performed many wedding ceremonies where there are two sets of parents for the bride or groom, and she has observed that many people are able to come together with a spirit of good will in the best interests of their children.

Finding Resources and Moving Ahead

Life is not always fair—there's no doubt about that. Sometimes a partner dies and leaves little or no insurance. Many men refuse to pay child support, and the system is not always efficient enough to rectify this situation. Too many men have abused their wives and children. By all means, a woman needs to do all she can to retrieve any support that is due her, and she needs to report and put a stop to any emotional or physical abuse that may be occurring. At the same time, she must refuse to allow herself to become a victim for any reason. She needs to teach her children that they are not victims, that they have within themselves the power to survive and thrive. There is no power in being a victim, but there IS power in doing everything possible each day to move ahead with life. Each small step forward provides the impetus for the next step forward. Each resource found and utilized gives one momentum. The following suggestions may give you, a female parent who is on her own, some ideas to start you on your way to a happier, more satisfying life:

1) Take advantage of your extended family: Not everyone is fortunate enough to have relatives who are willing and able

to be supportive. But when this is the case, it can be a life-saver. (For example, President Clinton's mother, Virginia Kelly, was able to leave him with her mother while she trained to be a nurse.)

2) Male role models can be accessed through YMCA programs, Big Brothers, the Boy Scouts, or other community organizations.

3) Parenting classes are available in most communities. If you can't find one in yours, ask your local PTA, school officials, or church to think about offering them.

4) Support groups for single parents, such as Parents Without Partners, can be found in most areas, and many churches have support groups for singles—check the Community Events section of your paper   If you can't find one to join, organize one yourself.

5) Check out parent cooperatives that offer child care. In a cooperative, a group of parents pool their resources. Each works a set number of hours caring for the children; then the parent is entitled to leave her children the same number of hours she has worked. If there is not a cooperative in your area, perhaps you could organize one. Even two or three parents sharing in this way can be very helpful.

6) Each community has its own unique resources. If there is a community college in your area, it may offer special programs for women and help in a variety of areas. Usually, if you find even one good resource, the people involved in it are aware of similar resources in the area. Don't be afraid to reach out and learn all you can about what might be available.

For example, in our local community in North Idaho, there is a Children's Village that reaches out to children and families in need.

Presently, there is room for 12 children in one big home, and another duplicate home is under construction. The Village takes in children for many reasons, such as abuse and neglect and homelessness, and they do some foster care for the state, but they also have taken care of children for shorter periods of time while their parents are re-establishing their lives in some way. (One woman left her three children there for a year-and-a-half.) While most of these cases stem from financial need, children may also be left for brief periods because a parent is psychologically unable to cope with the stress in her life and needs a temporary respite.

Parenting Skillfully

Ione has worked as a teacher and counselor in the early elementary education field and has counseled troubled parents as well. Her extensive experience in dealing with both generations has led her to a fascinating and significant conclusion about parenting: A parent with proficient skills will be successful in raising a child whether she is single or coupled. Similarly, an unskillful parent will face problems regardless of her marital state. The issue is not whether a parent is single or not, but whether the parent possesses the essentials for successful parenting—or, is at least open to developing those skills. But what are the most crucial abilities that will spell success? Some of them follow.

Boundaries

Children need adults to set limits for them and to provide consistency. Doing so provides a safe and secure structure for children's lives. House parents at Children's Village feel that parents' failure to set boundaries as well as parents' inconsistency in their disciplinary approach present major stumbling blocks that children must learn to overcome. So often, when an adult defines a boundary, and when a child pushes the limit of that boundary, the adult backs off. The child then begins to push every boundary he or she can, just to find out where the limits are. The more a parent fails to adhere to consistent boundaries and undeviating consequences for misbehavior, the more out of control the child becomes.

To be effective, boundaries must be fair and appropriate and not be based on a parent's irrational fears or unhealed areas from her own childhood. Children do outgrow specific boundaries, so changing them thoughtfully is not indicative of inconsistency, but is more characterisitic of a sense of fairness. It's important that children understand that boundaries can be changed or expanded after a thoughtful, careful exploration and discussion, but never as the result of temper tantrums. In this way, a parent can be just as clear about changing a boundary as setting one. It is also a good idea to allow children to participate in decisions whenever appropriate and to help them become as independent and self-actualizing as possible. At the same time, it's critical that the parent be the responsible adult who knows when to step in and take charge.

Ione's book, *Empowering the Child from Within: Education and Parenting for the 21st Century,* deals powerfully and persuasively with many areas of the parent-child relationship. She has successfully parented two boys, and she has taught and counseled children of all ages. The following example of a parent's failure to impose reasonable boundaries is taken from the "Walking the Line" chapter in Ione's book, which deals with empowering our children while still functioning responsibly as the adult in charge:

> While attending a child's Christmas program, I witnessed a good example of a parent's failure to impose appropriate boundaries. I overheard a small child about three years of age tell her mother that she did not want to

go up front and be in the program with the rest of the children. Since she didn't have a special part in the program, the mother wisely honored the child's right to decide and allowed her to say "no" to participation in the program. Up to that point, the mother was doing well.

However, after the program started, the mother allowed the child to run up and down the aisle, crawl on stage amid the performers, and noisily detract from the children who had chosen to participate. It was the child's right to decide about her own participation, but it was not her right to interfere with the rest of the program, nor to ruin it for everyone else! The mother should have intervened and removed her daughter to the back of the sanctuary, or even outside if necessary. The mother had the opportunity, which she ignored, to teach her child about choices, about other people's rights, and to show her child where individual freedom begins and ends. A child first understands these boundaries by having a responsible adult clearly set the limits about what behavior is acceptable and what is not. It's a prelude to learning how to set limits on his/her own behavior.

Loving and Caring

Another crucial element of parenting is giving a child all the love and understanding we possibly can. Children need hugs; they need to be told they are loved. They need to be assured of the fact that they are worthwhile and essentially good in spite of the fact that they occasionally misbehave. Adults need to be able to separate their children's behavior, which varies, from their innate goodness and light, which never deviates.

In order to be able to give children the love and care they need, a single mother must learn to balance her own needs with those of her children. She needs to know that it's not only all right, but essential, to take care of herself so that she will have adequate physical and emotional energy to give to her children. On the airlines, flight attendants always instruct parents with small children that should the need arise, they must place the oxygen mask over their own faces first and then help the child. Obviously, if a parent passes out for lack of oxygen, the child would not be helped at all. Neither can the children of a single mother be adequately nurtured and parented if that single mother isn't meeting, at the very least, her own fundamental physical and emotional needs.

When Julie divorced, she felt frightened, panic-stricken, empty, and abandoned. During the stressful time period that followed, she was diligent in making sure her children's physical demands were well taken care of, but she often found it difficult to be emotionally present with them due to her own inner turmoil and unmet needs. Later, after being in school and gaining more self-understanding, self-esteem, and support, she was able to function much better. She came to the realization that it was difficult to give her children the attention they needed and deserved while she was so stressed herself. The more a single mother can find ways to take care of herself in a healthy way and get the support she requires, the more nurturing and emotionally present she will be able to be with her children.

Finding or forming a support group, seeking out counseling, taking a parenting class, setting aside time to talk with friends or to be involved in a relaxing hobby are just some of the many ways to begin taking care of ourselves. It may be difficult to find the time, but it is essential to the well-being of both mother and child. The following stories illustrate some of the joys, sorrows, and challenges of single parenting and how different women have handled them.

Karen—Choosing Single Parenthood

Karen is the mother of a five-year-old son, Levi. She chose to give birth to a child and to parent that child on her own. She found herself in her mid-thirties with a pattern of unhealthy relationships and realized that she might never marry; yet she wanted a child of her own. At the time she made the decision to become pregnant, she was surrounded by supportive friends who wanted to help all they could. Since then, many of those friends have moved, so Karen is now quite alone with her responsibility.

Karen says that her biggest challenges are 1) financial, and 2) stress related—that is, the demands inherent in working, attending college classes, and looking after her son. In spite of the many pressures, though, she manages to find constructive ways to deal with her problems. She buys clothes at thrift shops, toys and games at garage sales, and is always on the lookout for a bargain. She finds a way to make sure that her son's material needs are met. In spite of her stress and long hours, Karen and Levi are able to maintain a close and loving relationship. She is good at setting limits and showering love at the same time. They have a space in their basement with big plastic balls and a bat. Either of them can go there to defuse any frustrations; it's okay to scream, hit balls, or pound the walls. Karen is adept at explaining things to Levi, and he knows that he is a loved and very important person in his mother's life. He is a sweet-natured, well-behaved child who relates well with other children and adults. Although Karen says she didn't realize what a tremendous amount of energy it would take to single-parent a child, she is happy to be a mother and says, "I don't regret my choice for a minute!"

Vera—A Widow's Unskillful Sacrifice

Vera and Bud married right out of high school. They were very much in love, and Bud worked in construction, while Vera stayed home and had five babies. Since there were always pressing financial needs, and because Bud was only in his early thirties, not much thought was given to life insurance. When Bud took ill with a fast-growing cancer and died within months, Vera was left with five children, ages one through twelve. She survived the best she could on Social Security, and when all the children were in school, she went to work as a waitress. During all this time, she lived for her children, denying them nothing, and always finding an excuse for any unacceptable behavior on their part. She did not date, for she didn't meet anyone who was willing to take on several children, and besides, Vera was not comfortable with the idea of a stepfather for the children. After the children were grown, she finally married a man who loved her and had been waiting for her to say yes for several years. All went well for a while, until the untenable behavior of two of the children, who had learned to be very demanding of their mother, caused the marriage to break up. Vera now lives with her youngest son. Two of Vera's children became very self-sufficient, productive people. The other three have had continuing problems supporting themselves, with two having spent some time in jail. If Vera had taken better care of herself instead of becoming a martyr, if she had set reasonable but firm boundaries for her children, if she had expected them to be more self-sufficient and responsible, perhaps the outcome could have been less painful.

Debbie—Surviving Against All Odds

Debbie divorced her abusive husband five years ago, but she has never been able to collect the child support that is due her. At the time of the divorce, there were five children, seven through fifteen years of age. Debbie was on welfare for a while, but went through a training program at the local community college and found work. She continues to try to collect the child support, but her ex-husband continually finds ways to get out of it. He tells the authorities that he has no money and that he is living out of his truck, but this is not truly the case. In spite of all this hardship, Debbie and her five children are doing quite well. She has supportive family members who live in the area, and she has made use of the resources available to her. Her youngest son, now 12, is active in scouting and holds a part-time job as well. Her 18-year-old son just left for the Marines. Her oldest child, a daughter, is now 20, married, and living away from home. Her 15-year-old son is learning disabled, but is attending school and doing well. Her 16-year-old boy is a fine student and a football player. The boys are all progressing very nicely, with no signs of drug or alcohol problems. In spite of the many challenges, Debbie is managing to bring up her children by herself in an admirable way. Perhaps one reason for her success is her skill at setting boundaries and encouraging self-sufficiency.

Lee—Learning, Growing, Succeeding

Lee has raised her daughter Alicia by herself ever since she divorced Alicia's father shortly after Alicia's birth. Alicia is now 12 and doing beautifully. Lee has experienced financial challenges over the years, but she has been fortunate that Alicia's father has paid child support and has taken an interest in his daughter. Lee managed to stay at home with Alicia for her first two-and-a-half years by finding things she could do at home to earn income that supplemented the child support. Because her father lives several hours away, Alicia spends only two or three weeks a year with him. As a result, Lee feels burdened at times, as she is carrying most of the responsibility. However, Lee says one of her biggest challenges is to allow Alicia to be her own person, to accept her feelings for what they are, to listen and not always give solutions, and to allow Alicia to work problems out for herself as much as possible. Since Lee is aware of her tendency to overprotect, she has taken steps to overcome this problem. Over the years, she has been consistent in setting limits, but has then expanded them when appropriate. She is teaching Alicia to listen to her intuition—her own inner knowing that tells her what is right. Lee is a mother who works on her own psychological and spiritual growth and finds ways to help her daughter grow as well. Thus far, she has been very successful.

Susan—Finding a Workable Alternative

Susan is a divorced mother with two young boys, one of whom has a serious heart problem and has undergone several major surgeries. Susan wanted to be home with her boys, at least until school age. Because she had some training in the field of education and since she loves children and relates well to them, she found a way to stay at home and still earn the necessary money to supplement the child support she receives. Susan has turned her home into a small day-care center where she cares for up to six children besides her own. Some of these children just attend the center part-time or after school hours.

Even though Susan does receive child support from her ex-husband, she still feels the financial crunch. Fortunately, she has a family support system nearby and with their occasional help, has managed to deal successfully with the unexpected. She is comfortable with the choice she has made, and she knows the value of showing love to her children and the need to set reasonable boundaries. In addition to skillfully parenting her own boys, she is providing a loving and safe environment for other children as well.

Rose—A Triumph over Martyrdom

Rose is a young widow with a ten-year-old son named Jerry. She had a very difficult time when her husband Bruce died two years ago, first dealing with her grief, and then coping with her sense of isolation. Bruce and Rose had just moved to a large city to take better jobs and hadn't made close friends before Bruce was killed in an auto accident. Since Rose had always placed the needs of her family first, she had no idea how to begin to take care of herself. Rose sank into depression and martyrdom, using every ounce of her diminishing energy after work to focus upon the needs of her son. But, her inability to take care of herself led to a deeper and deeper depression. Jerry started to develop problems at school and felt that in many ways he had lost both his parents. To make matters worse, Rose's mental state was affecting her performance at work to such a degree that she realized she'd better get into counseling or risk losing her job. This decision to take action on her own behalf was a turning point for her.

In counseling over the past year, Rose has been doing her grief work and learning about the importance of caring for herself. She has arranged for Jerry to get the counseling he needs and has become a more active and emotionally present parent to her son. She is continuing her counseling sessions, attends a single-parent support group at her church, has made new friends, and is beginning to feel more hopeful about her future. Rose's story is a reminder that we must take charge of our lives by seeking out available resources and using them. In the process, we will become more fully functioning human beings and more skillful parents as well.

Life Is Not Always a Picture Book

Breathes there a mother with a soul so dead that she has not yearned for the perfect family? Perhaps one like the Waltons or Ozzie and Harriet's or the Cleavers? Perhaps one like the family down the street, who look like they have it all together? When we compare ourselves to a standard of perfection, we're bound to come up short. It is true that many parents in America need all the help they can get and then must commit themselves to using that assistance to become better parents. Once that modus operandi is in effect, however, it's important to have a wider perspective that includes the understanding that sometimes no matter how loving and skillful a parent might be, the outcome is not always what that parent might choose.

The wider perspective is the understanding that children have minds and souls of their own; there is always an unpredictability factor. There are no guarantees, but the odds that children will turn out to be productive human beings improve when they have at least one skillful parent. But even with good parenting, children will live out their own agenda, since each human being born on this planet (with the purpose, we believe, of attending and learning from Earth School) is a very special and unique soul. Many children raised in the worst of circumstances with terrible parents, turn out to be wonderful, compassionate, successful human beings. Some children raised in the best of circumstances, with loving parents, emerge as selfish, destructive human beings, sometimes even criminals.

There is much that can be done and should be done when it comes to caring for and guiding children, and if more adults were more adept as parents, role models, and boundary setters, no doubt the plight of the youth in our country would improve. Yet, as mentioned above, each child must find his or her own path. We believe this is what the poet Kahlil Gibran meant when he wrote in *The Prophet:* "Your children are not your children. They are the sons and daughters of Life's longing for itself. They come through you but not from you, and though they are with you yet they belong not to you." Because our children come through us, we certainly have a responsibility to provide them with the very best upbringing possible. Once we've done that, we must release ourselves from any guilt or regret about not being "perfect." There is no parent that is or ever was perfect, so we must be comforted by the knowledge that our children will proceed with the lessons their soul has chosen. And they will experience those lessons, with or without our permission. Once we understand this concept, we can be more compassionate toward ourselves and other parents as well. The following stories illustrate the fact that, even with loving and skillful parenting, things don't always turn out as we might wish.

Pat—Making a Difference Where She Can

Pat always thought she would marry, but it simply never happened. She became a social worker and a missionary in Brazil. While she was there, she rescued an abandoned baby boy that surely would have died if not for her efforts. She intended to nurse the child back to health, then find a parent for him in Brazil, but she gradually came to the realization that she loved him, and so she brought him back to the States with her and adopted him. With her mother's help, she raised him in a small-town environment where he received much love and support. David was a handsome and sweet boy, and all went well in his early years. However, by the time he reached high school age, he was difficult to handle, and he began drinking excessively. He married right out of high school, and he and his wife both had problems with alcohol. They had two boys before they divorced. David has had a difficult time holding a job and has had a difficult relationship with his own children. Conditions at home have been chaotic for these boys, so Pat has stepped in to become a loving and active grandparent—this, in spite of the fact that she had to retire early because of the cancer that is threatening her life.

Pat has sought counseling for both herself and her grandsons, which helps them better deal with the challenge of their parents' addiction. Pat's cancer is in remission right now, but no one knows for how long this will be the case. In the meantime, Pat is living as fully as she can in spite of her disappointment over her son's lifestyle and her concern about the eventual fate of her grandchildren. She maintains a close and loving relationship with her grandsons and has no regrets about her decision to become a single parent. While Pat wishes that her son's life could be more productive, she still loves him; at the same time she is releasing him to learn from the consequences of his own behavior.

Laura—After You've Done Your Best...

Laura's husband left her for another woman when their daughter LeeAnn was about seven. Laura was a compassionate person and a good mother who decided to go back to school and become a high school English teacher. LeeAnn and her mother were close during her growing years, and they seemed to exemplify a perfect picture. They lived comfortably, if not lavishly, and LeeAnn was well-dressed, popular, outgoing, and sensitive. Being brought up by a single mother seemed to bear no ill effects.

After high school, LeeAnn married a young man from a very strict, religious family who made some judgments about Laura's single status and the fact that she dated and was looking for another husband. When Laura married a divorced man that LeeAnn's in-laws did not approve of, LeeAnn eventually closed Laura out of her life. Laura continues to be happily remarried, but in spite of all her efforts to reconcile with her daughter, LeeAnn continues to reject her. Laura endures the heartbreak of being estranged not only from her daughter but from her two grandchildren as well. However, she chooses to make the best of her situation. Her spiritual life is of primary importance to her, providing comfort and a broader perspective.

M. Scott Peck, M.D., begins his bestselling book, *The Road*

Less Traveled, with this sentence: "Life is difficult." He goes on to make the point that once we accept that fact and decide to get on with our lives in spite of our difficulties, we are then able to transcend them. Working through this process is a task for all of us. As we deal with the challenges in our lives, it's comforting to know that we're not alone, that there is support out there, that there is hope.

In the final analysis, the more a parent is able to refrain from attaching a specific life picture to a child, the better for both parent and child. One woman we know feels that she very successfully raised two sons. One is married, has a steady job, and is a fine and kind and loving person. The other son is unmarried, has a good job, a keen mind, and is also a fine and loving person. He happens to be gay and HIV positive, but he is using that experience to grow and is meeting his challenges with wisdom and courage. Our friend is equally proud of her two sons, and feels they both have been successfully parented.

Our job is to be the best parent we know how to be and then to know that the child will have his/her own agenda for learning and growing. When we plant a rosebush, we try to furnish good soil, water it, and give it adequate light, but then we stand back, and it grows at its own pace and produces its unique blossoms—but only when and if it's ready. So it is with our children.

❖ SUMMING UP ❖

One of the most awesome responsibilities we ever take on is that of parenting, and when a woman finds herself alone with that challenge, she is often overwhelmed at first. However, there is help and hope for the mother who refuses to allow herself to play the victim role. A single woman can successfully parent her children if 1) she is determined to utilize all the resources available to her, 2) she is willing to work to heal her own anger and resentment toward the father of her children, and 3) she is willing to take care of herself by working on her own psychological and spiritual healing and growth.

Action Steps

◆ Hug your children at least once a day and tell them you love them. Never get too busy to forget doing so!

◆ Make a list of age-appropriate boundaries for each child and stick to them. When they are no longer applicable, be open to extending them.

◆ On a regular basis, make time (even for one hour) to do something special with each of your children. This special time could involve reading, playing a game, talking over the child's concerns, taking a walk, and so on.

◆ At least once a week, take time to do something special just for you. This time might entail attending a counseling session or a support group, going to the gym, having lunch with a friend, relaxing with a good book, or going to a matinee. (If you can't afford a sitter, see if you can "trade time" with another mother.)

◆ Make a list of the resources that are available to you. Review the resources listed in this chapter, and add any new ones that you can think of.

◆ Seek out and participate in a single-parent support group. Check area churches, the YWCA, women's centers, and Parents Without Partners. If none are available in your area, think about starting one yourself!

◆ Take a parenting class. These are offered periodically by church groups, the YWCA, and women's centers. Watch your local newspaper for the next one in your area. (Those in the medical or psychological fields in your city or town might also be able to direct you to such classes.)

◆ Affirm often: *"I love, nurture, and respect myself. I love, nurture, and respect my children. Together we move forward into our highest good as a family."*

❖ ❖ ❖

CHAPTER SEVEN

AGING WITH PRIDE AND POWER

"Getting older is an adventure, not a problem!"

— Betty Friedan

Many countries do a much better job providing for the elderly than the United States does. The Scandinavians, for example, have an approach called Open Care, which encourages and helps older people to live in their own homes. This program enables the elderly to stay in familiar surroundings when they might otherwise have been sent to nursing homes (where people often lose individuality, dignity, and any control over their lives). It is our fervent hope that, in time, America will address the issues of aging in a more helpful way than in the past, and certainly, Scandinavian countries could teach us much about what works well. However, until the U.S. Government makes the issues affecting older citizens a priority, we must take matters into our own hands. Although aging Americans are becoming more politically active and are trying to change the system, we need to be innovative in establishing and maintaining our individual lifestyles, and we need to seek out ways to meet our own unique requirements.

Early in American history, it was a part of the natural evolution of life for families to care for the older generation. Many homes in America prior to World War II were three-generational households or, at the very least, large extended families who lived near each other and who watched out for one another. Mobility was much more rare in those days, and people lived in the same town with any number of sisters, brothers, aunts, uncles, cousins, and grandparents.

As Ione was growing up, her constant playmate and friend from birth through high school, Thelma June Dawson, lived in a three-generational household. There was Thelma, her older sister Carol, her parents, her unmarried Aunt Dorothy, and her grandmother, Herweg. Aunt Dorothy and Grandmother Herweg had moved in temporarily during the Depression. Mr. Dawson was out of work, and Mrs. Dawson couldn't provide enough income as a teacher, so Mrs. Dawson's relatives moved in to help with expenses.

Eventually, Aunt Dorothy developed mental health problems that left her hospitalized for two decades, and Grandma Herweg came to live with the Dawsons permanently. That was how many families handled the issue of elderly relatives.

Although Ione never lived under the same roof with relatives outside her immediate family, she was part of a large and supportive extended family. Her grandparents lived in their own old house and were the parents of ten living children. All their children and grandchildren lived in the same town of about 25,000 people, and everyone came to check up on Grandma and Grandpa O'Hara at least once or twice a week. When Grandpa was in his final months of life, bedridden and requiring 24-hour care, his children divided up the night shift and some of the daytime hours; everyone took their turn helping Grandma care for him. There was never a question of whether they would help or not. Everyone just pitched in and did their share. That's just the way it was!

Unfortunately, modern life has made the solutions and remedies of the past—when it comes to caring for the elderly—less viable. Our peripatetic natures have created great geographical distances among many family members. Other factors also enter into the feasibility of children caring for elderly parents. In most preretirement households, both adults are employed full-time, so the woman is not able to become the primary caretaker for an aging or a disabled parent, whether hers or her mate's.

Shorter life spans prior to the second half of the 20th century meant that people often died early and only required care for a few years at most. These days, with medical care much more advanced, many people are living into their eighties and nineties and even beyond. Unfortunately, this extension of life does not always mean that the *quality* of life is extended accordingly, as many elderly people have greatly diminished physical and mental processes, making it impossible to live and function on their own. Even in those cases where it would be physically possible for an older person to live alone, if the minimal thinking skills required for independent living are so inadequate as to require constant supervision (as with those who have Alzheimer's disease), alternative living situations are mandatory. Masil's mother, Grace, who lives with us here at the Holo Center, is in that very position. Fortunately, we don't have to program ourselves for a difficult time as we age. We can choose to take charge of our future. We can choose to age with pride and power instead of allowing ourselves to become victims.

Planning Ahead: A Jump Start

One way to empower ourselves is to prepare for our financial and housing needs as early as we can. We can build or alter our living spaces to more comfortably accommodate us during our later years. Here at the Holo Center our doorways are extra wide. One bathroom with its oversized shower and hand-held shower spray can easily accommodate a wheelchair. The sink is also low and wheelchair accessible. Light switches are within easy reach, and push switches would make them even easier to operate.

Other suggestions for making homes more "elder-friendly" are levers instead of doorknobs, safety treads for stairs and tubs, handrails, and easy-to-read thermostats and telephone dials. Most of these modifications would only require simple alterations, but they can make life much easier for women as they age. However, the time to make such changes is when we are healthy and physically fit. Then, we can relax, knowing we have done everything we can to allow us to live in our own homes as long as possible. As you read about some women who decided to take charge of their own futures, you might think about your own elder years and what you can do to prepare for them.

Elsie—Choosing for Herself

Some women who are alone and childless take even further measures to prepare for a time when they may need other living arrangements. Elsie was living alone, and although robust and very healthy up into her later seventies, she determined she wanted to make her own decisions and choices about where she would live if and when she was no longer able to live in her own house. She spent two or three years looking at several possible alternatives. When she finally found a retirement complex that felt just right, she proceeded to take the necessary steps to ensure that a living space would be available when she was ready. After that task was accomplished, she began the process of going through her house and deciding what she would take with her to her new home and just what things needed to be disposed of and to whom they would go. She moved slowly and deliberately through each step of the process, and then she decided to make the move while she was still healthy and active. She had time to adjust, form new friendships, and make certain she would be properly cared for if she became unable to care for herself.

Hollie—Flexible Living

Hollie, another woman alone who had no immediate family, moved into a similar retirement complex. The building she lives in has an infirmary where she recently stayed after she broke her leg in a fall. Not requiring hospitalization, yet not ready for independent living, she was able to recuperate in the infirmary until she healed sufficiently to return to her own apartment. A long-term care unit for those with more serious needs is also part of the complex.

Both Hollie and Elsie have adequate financial resources that made it possible for them to select from excellent options. Not everyone has such a wide selection of choices available, but there are more alternatives than we might think.

Emily—Exploring Low-Income Alternatives

Low-rent government subsidized housing is available in many cities. Emily, an elderly, widowed aunt of Ione's, moved into one of these apartment complexes several years ago. Many of her friends and acquaintances from over the years were living there as well, and they all proceeded to spend many happy hours together. Since these women had all married young and raised children, many of them had never appreciated the freedom they enjoyed in the later years of their lives. The friendship and camaraderie they had shared with one another for over 50 years continued for as long as they all lived, and Ione is certain that her Aunt Emily lived a longer and more rewarding life than she would have lived in her own home, where she was afraid to be alone.

Emily had her own small apartment where she could cook her

own meals, but she also had the option of eating in the community dining room. In the activity room, the residents could do crafts, play cards or bingo, or just sit and visit. Lovely courtyards and lawn furniture provided opportunities to sit outdoors during fair weather. Some of Emily's friends still maintained their own cars, and they often invited her and others to go on shopping trips or to go out to eat. These women had some glorious times during those final years of their lives, and they had the freedom to enjoy themselves in ways that were totally novel to them. Also, if one of the women was not feeling well or hadn't been seen or heard from for a few hours, someone always checked up on her. More than once when Ione went to pick her aunt up to take her somewhere, she'd say: "I need to let one of the 'girls' know where I'm going so they won't worry."

Mutual Support Through Shared Housing

Estelle Getty, the actress who played Sophia on the popular TV program, *The Golden Girls,* was quoted in an interview as saying: "I've always felt loneliness—not age—is the real killer." To a large degree, that statement is accurate. Statistics point out that single people, including widows and widowers, die younger than do their married counterparts. But the issue isn't the piece of legal paper; the issue is caring and companionship. From the very core of our being, our souls seem to have a basic need for warmth, love, and companionship, just as the physical body needs food, clothing, and shelter to sustain it.

Another statistic: Being widowed, divorced, separated or never married dramatically increases a woman's chance of living in poverty in her old age. When a woman is trying to survive with very limited resources, it is all too easy for her to succumb to feelings of deprivation and depression, but we need to remember that there are viable alternatives. Often, an older woman's limited resources are tied up in housing. For example, one in three women 65 and older spends more than half of her income on rent. Female homeowners spend 40 percent or more of their income on housing costs.

There is a way out of this trap, and that way is shared housing (see Chapter Two). By sharing a living space, a woman can cut her expenses in half! This living arrangement is also a way to build a network of caring people who will help each other when needed. Some women resist this course of action because they want to know that everything is just exactly where they want it in the kitchen and elsewhere in their home. They don't want to adapt to living with others. The question that needs to be asked is, "Is it more important for me to have my forks perfectly arranged in the silverware drawer, or is it more important for me to be involved with other human beings in a mutually beneficial fashion?" Women who live with others stay healthier and are obviously less lonely. Yes, there are issues that need to be worked out between people who live together, and it's important to find compatible housemates, but with some effort and investigation, it can be done. It is a mistake to allow this alternative to go unexplored.

Old Age Isn't for Sissies

Many older women know from first-hand experience that "old age isn't for sissies," but product designer Patricia Moore made that clear to everyone by disguising herself as an 80-year-old woman and going out into the world to do research on how people treat the elderly. She was often treated as a hindrance and a nuisance; people slammed doors in her face, verbally abused her, patronized her, and assumed she was deaf and ignorant. She had three wardrobes—for a poor, middle-class, and affluent woman, respectively, but she found that she was treated with equal disdain no matter how she was dressed. In some cases, people treated her with kindness, but those were the exceptions. Unfortunately, many young Americans buy into the age stereotype and don't want to be bothered or inconvenienced by the elderly. It's no wonder that as we approach our elder years, we often do it with so much resistance, fear, and apprehension!

Masil, the "golden girl" who lives with us in community, is 72. Last fall, the pickup truck she was driving was hit in the rear, pushed off into the trees, and totaled. If Masil hadn't been wearing her seat belt, she would have been badly injured. As it was, she hit her head on the windshield and was dazed. She was taken by ambulance to the emergency room of our local hospital where her confusion persisted. When Ione went to the emergency room to be with her and to sign any necessary papers (we have legal documents giving each of us the right to make medical decisions for one another should one of us become incapable of making them for herself), the doctors were ready to discharge Masil in spite of her obviously disoriented state. Why? Because with her gray hair and wrinkles and advanced age, they assumed that she was always dazed and confused! If Ione hadn't been there to set the doctors straight and insist on proper tests and procedures, Masil could have been discharged with a concussion or other serious injury. No, old age isn't for sissies; it presents a set of formidable challenges. However, in spite of these obstacles, we can choose to seek out creative and empowering strategies; we can insist on aging with dignity. We can, as author and metaphysical teacher Louise Hay says, be "elders of excellence." We must not meekly give up the power to control our own fate.

Aging Proudly

Columnist Ellen Goodman believes that our image-conscious culture actually hinders women from aging proudly and gracefully. Public attention is focused on those who are "still" attractive at 50 or 60 or even 70 (often with the help of cosmetic surgery). Our culture offers women ways to extend their looks so they can try to look younger longer, but women are not given permission to proudly claim their true age. Famous women such as Katharine Hepburn and the late Jessica Tandy—admirable role models for us all—have just gone ahead and aged proudly anyway!

We are just at that in-between stage of life. Later middle age? Early old age? We find ourselves very sensitive to attitudes toward age and aging. Julie recently spent time with her 86-year-old mother, Mary, who lives in Michigan. Mary's mind is sound, but her body is frail, and she has trouble with her eyesight. Recently widowed, she moved to the Detroit area to be near Julie's brothers. Very social and outgoing and interested in making new friends, Mary was looking forward to checking out the Senior Citizens Center in the area during Julie's visit, so Julie arranged for the Center's van to pick up her and her mother for a pre-Christmas luncheon. The van driver was a senior volunteer, very able, affable, and well liked by the eight regular riders. The seniors, of various ages, were quite friendly and all concerned for one another's welfare. This sojourn was Julie's first experience with a senior group, and in some ways she felt like a "senior in disguise"; yet, she realized that she did indeed "qualify" as one. After lunch, a woman of about 45 sang and led the seniors in Christmas carols. The woman seemed to be talking down to the group as if these people were children in kindergarten, and Julie definitely felt included! She began to understand in a very real way how easy it is to get caught up in the "old-age" stereotype and to eventually accept the "less-than" perception of others. Aging with pride and power seems to require a great deal of self-esteem, as well as the determination not to allow others to devalue us just because we happen to be older.

Aging Powerfully

There is no time limit on creativity and zest for life. The gifted choreographer Martha Graham asserted at the age of 81: "I know some women of 16 who are old. They have settled themselves very nicely, and that's going to be the height of their adventure. I'm still hungry for every sensation I can get." The most powerful tools we have at our disposal no matter what our age, are our minds, our attitudes, our power to choose. We can embrace and investigate new ways of being and doing. Betty Friedan, in *The Fountain of Age,* reminds us that the last years of life provide the opportunity for NEW development, for FURTHER evolution of our minds and souls; it does not have to be a time of decline and deterioration! Those who are dynamically aging have a perpetual sense of adventure and an enthusiastic acceptance of change. They realize that their remaining time is limited, and they want to make the most of it; they want to take full advantage of the opportunities that arise. They continue to set goals and to work toward them with gusto.

The television news magazine *20/20* receives repeated requests to air their special program on women who are still vital and active even when they are over 100 years old. The reporters concluded that these women shared four common characteristics: optimism, engagement, mobility, and the ability to handle loss and go on in spite of it.

Engagement—that is, the ability to be involved in life—is perhaps the most essential ingredient because it keeps us optimistic and mobile, and it gives the impetus to move forward in spite of loss. It allows us to remain open and willing to experiment with different activities until we find what is right for us. When a woman is engaged with life, she values herself and others through love, friendship, compassion, and sometimes even indignation.

The specific nature of a woman's involvement will depend on her personality. For example, a clown organization comprised of older people goes out into children's hospitals to cheer the young patients. A senior symphony orchestra, entirely composed of retired musicians, donates its performances to charitable causes. There is an outdoor organization for women in Salt Lake City called the Great Old Broads for Wilderness. These women embark on a long trek into the wilderness at least once a year; their mission is to preserve undeveloped areas and to abolish the myth that only the young can enjoy strenuous exercise. If we will just look around us, we will find numerous opportunities to work creatively, to study, to volunteer, to be a part of life. Nonagenarian comedian George Burns summed it up when he said, "How can I die? I'm booked."

It's comforting for those women entering, or already well into, elderhood to know that many women have done their most remarkable work in their sixties, seventies, eighties, and even nineties. One can be inspired by the many women, both living and deceased, who have kept engaged and who have never allowed age to limit them. Margaret Mead, Georgia O'Keeffe, Golda Meir, Indira Gandhi, Helen Hayes, Jessica Tandy, Louise Hay, May Sarton, Katharine Hepburn, Margaret Chase Smith, Eleanor Roosevelt, and Betty Friedan are just a few of them. We can also be inspired by those women we know personally who aren't well known but who provide us with models of courage, compassion, and vitality. Some examples of strong, empowered women follow.

Vitally Alive and Dancing

Mary Krenk is a women in her seventies who is a wonderful model of vigor, enthusiasm, and compassion. She and her husband Marv volunteer their time and talents to the Eugene, and Springfield, Oregon Senior Centers as teachers of International Folk Dance. Their zeal bubbled over as they spoke with us about the joy that they experience each week during their dance sessions, not to mention the delight of the participants. Ninety percent of the "students" are single women, ranging in age from 48 to 87. Because Mary and Marv are seniors themselves, they treat those in the group as the equals they are. There is no "talking down." Everyone is very kind and patient with one another, but the expectation is that people will learn the dances, the history behind them, and something about the culture from which each dance originates. Mary and Marv see the level of each participant's confidence rise each week as they endeavor to exercise both their brains and their bodies. They see dispositions improve and more smiles appear as people get to know each other and then extend their friendships outside the dancing classes. They told us, "There is almost something mystical about what happens between the people (mostly older women) who participate." Mary and Marv presented us with the following poem, which expresses the feelings of many who dance:

CIRCLE

Where else do we touch
more than one another,
other than kin,
at any one time;
in this grownup world,

after school is thru,
after clans are gone,
after tribes are lost,
after villages are swallowed?
Where but in a circle
when but in dance
from other lands,
or past times
(when people still touched,
before clans, tribes, towns
were vanished away)?
Where but in circles
do we feel flesh on both sides;
see it link around
thru a stood multitude
of bodies like our own
'till it connects us back?
Thru all these people
we touch ourselves,
and are touched
by a Family vaster
than we knew we had.

— Gordon Yaswen

Women alone need to know there is a vast extended family out there; all we need do is reach out and access that family through whatever avenue feels comfortable to us. Classes and activities are available at senior centers in nearly every community in the United States. If you don't relate to a specific class or teacher, don't give up—try again! International Folk Dance is taught throughout the United States, so if your senior center doesn't currently offer it, perhaps you could be the one to initiate classes (or offer to teach them yourself). [4]

Embracing Eldership: Adventures in Aging

Julie's Perspective

Like many women, I've always thought aging was what happened to others. Although I've always admired women who aged well and dynamically, I always pictured myself as "one of the younger ones." As I approached my 60th birthday, the realization hit me: I'm no longer "one of the younger ones!" I don't have forever! My time is limited, and I'd better make the most of it! That's when I decided to retire from full-time church ministry and to get back into free-lancing, which gives me the opportunity to be active and involved, but at a more relaxed and even pace. The first thing I did was get to work on finishing my autobiography. Although I've self-published it and sold many copies, it doesn't seem likely to become a bestseller. Nonetheless, it is one of the most productive things I've ever done. My experience with this endeavor has led me to believe that just about anyone would benefit from writing their own story. It provided me with the chance to review my life, to gain perspective, and to grasp a sense of what my life adds up to. It gave me the opportunity to ask and answer the questions: What have I learned? What have I left undone or unhealed that I need to take care of? What was the meaning and purpose of the painful times? Why did I make the choices I did? Just telling my story has been a healing experience for me, and many women who have read the book tell me that it's been healing for them as well. I'm happy that

---

[4] A Folk Dance directory is available for $10 from The Society of Folk Dance Historians, 2100 Rio Grande, Austin, TX 78705-5513. Phone (512) 478-8900. Poetry packet $5 from Gordon Yaswen, 740 First St., Sebastopol, CA 95472.

I gave myself the gift of time to complete that writing project. Along with the writing came the opportunity to learn a new skill— word processing on the computer—which just shows that an old dog or an old woman can learn new tricks!

Two well-known older women have been role models for me: the acclaimed artist Grandma Moses, and the founder of the Gray Panthers, Maggie Kuhn. When I was feeling old, starting college from scratch at 32, I remembered that Grandma Moses didn't start painting until she was well into her sixties and didn't become recognized until she was over 70. She continued to paint, improving all the while, until she was over 100 years old. I thought, "If Grandma Moses can do it, so can I!" Now that I'm over 60 myself, I thank Grandma Moses for the inspiration to move ahead with my writing. Sixty is still young!

Maggie Kuhn is now in her eighties. When she was forced to retire from her social work position at 65, she organized the Gray Panthers, a group of men and women who fight age discrimination and other social injustices. Several years ago, I attended a conference on aging sponsored by Esalen Institute, where Maggie was one of the featured speakers. Feisty, energetic, intelligent, committed to living life fully, she has lived in community for several years with a varied group of people. She inspires me, and many other women as well, to live our lives fully engaged; she demonstrates that there is life after retirement and that it never needs to be boring!

However, without the responsibility of a full-time ministry, I find that I must be more self-directed. I have to find reasons inside myself for getting up in the morning; I have to set up my own tasks and creative endeavors. They are not laid out before me in a job description, nor do people appear before me every day in need of prayer and direction. I have time for introspection and am able to take a closer look at my own inner processes. I am finally accepting my physical body—wrinkles, flab, and all. I try to eat health-fully and exercise and take care of myself in every way I can, but I am no longer concerned about how attractive I am compared to Liz Taylor, who happens to be my age. I know that I have a body, but I am much more than my body. After all the years of angst spent con-cerned over how I looked and the years of worrying about what other people thought of my appearance, it is a tremendous relief to be free of that albatross around my neck. I believe that this attitude is one of the perks of getting older and accepting the inevitable. When I was younger, I thought that when the time came for a face lift, I'd get one if I could possibly afford it. But now I feel I've earned every wrinkle, or perhaps more accurately, character line. What my face has become is a reflection of who I am becoming, and I'm really okay with it.

I noticed in the newspaper under "celebrity birthdays" that Elizabeth Taylor and Joanne Woodward share the same February birthday. At the time, Elizabeth was 62 and Joanne was 64. Elizabeth is an example of a woman who gets face lifts and fights age every step of the way. Joanne, on the other hand, exemplifies the woman who does not resort to face lifts and who seems com-fortable with the natural process of aging. I've always admired Elizabeth's independence and tendency to live life "her way" in spite of public criticism. I admire her courage and respect her deci-sion to get cosmetic surgery if that is what she chooses, but I won-der if she isn't a prisoner of her own image as a "great beauty." I suspect that Joanne's natural acceptance of age makes her more content in the long run, and she serves as a role model for me.

Along with the acknowledgment of what is naturally happening to my body, I am accepting myself in other ways as well. I'm embracing the attitude of Popeye: "I am what I am and that's all that I am!" For years I had a pressing urge to prove to myself and others that I was worthy...to be alive? At long last I've worked through that. My autobiography is basically the story of why I felt the way I did, what blind alleys I walked down to fix it, and a description of the processes that finally led to peace and acceptance. However, I know that I'm not finished yet. I am aware that life itself is a continuous flow. As long as we're alive, we're in process. My goal is to "live till I die." I want to continue to move forward, to keep learning new ways to love. I want to grow in patience, understanding, wisdom, and compassion. I embrace this phase of my life and realize that it just may be the grandest adventure of them all!

Ione's Perspective

"I looked into the mirror today, and for the first time I realized that my physical immortality is in jeopardy!"

One morning at the ripe old age of 56, I awakened from the dream state with those words running through my mind. I grabbed my pen and wrote them down. When I finished, I had to chuckle, wondering from what depth of my being those words had emerged. Up to that point, I had given very little thought to the process of aging; it still seemed like something in the dim and distant future. Because I was enjoying excellent health, was happy, and living life "my way," I hadn't thought about getting old anytime soon! However, now the facts were inescapable, and I found that thoughts of getting older were floating around in my conscious mind as I moved through my daily life.

I found myself wondering: What will my later years look like? Will I remain healthy? Are there ways to help ensure that I will be? Will I be alone? Are there ways I can prepare for, or avoid, that eventuality? Will my financial resources be sufficient? What are my alternatives if it isn't? Will my family survive me? Who can I count on if they don't?

I soon realized that we can make as many arrangements as possible, take as many steps as we can to ensure a quality eldership for ourselves, and this is certainly the wise thing to do, but even after all that preparation, we have to accept that there will always be an unknown quantity. Here is where I find that my faith and inner strength have to come into play. Ultimately, my only true security lies in a personal faith in Divine Order (God) and in my capacity to face the unexpected. I must rely on my creative ability to cope with adversity and to seek ways to find meaning, even when there appears to be none. This is a skill I work on constantly! It is a process that must permeate our lives on a day-to-day basis in order for us to draw on it when needed.

As I enter my period of eldership, I confront the limitations of finite time. I don't have forever, in this particular incarnation, to enjoy the world around me. I'm trying harder to "BE HERE NOW" and smell more roses, delight in more frivolous acts of humor, allow myself to be more outrageous in a kindly and nonharmful manner, and not be concerned about impressing anyone. I have stopped worrying, as my mother used to, about "what the neighbors will think" and now concentrate only on being more loving, supportive, and nonjudgmental to those around me. I don't always succeed, but I am consciously working on it.

One question which frequently arises is: "What will I do with the time left? How do I wish to be known when it's over?" The American Olympic Figure Skating gold medalists often ask themselves, "Have I added something to the sport and left it better than it was before I came along?" I would like to be able to substitute "life" for "the sport" and then answer that question with a resounding YES!

I think that the realization that one is aging is a little like finding out that we have a terminal illness—it gives us an opportunity to stop and reflect and evaluate our lives. It has given me time to confront death, and to work out my feelings with myself and with those I love. It has helped me discover just what I believe as opposed to the myths or rote religious training of my early years.

Also, this process has afforded me the wisdom to appreciate many things that I'd overlooked before. Because I now realize that time is limited, I spend more time with people I love and less time on meaningless pursuits. I have a much greater appreciation for little things like the handmade quilt my mother-in-law gave me as a young bride with all the intricate stitches and the hours of labor and love that went into its making. I value more and more deeply my trips to the spectacular Oregon coast as it dawns on me that there will be a finite number of them left to enjoy this time around.

I don't take things as seriously as I once did, and yet, I find that I have a greater awareness of the need to take care of this little planet of ours, a small sphere in a black space with nowhere else to go. I'd like future generations to know and enjoy this wonderful, beautiful, natural world, as I have. I would like my grown children and my younger friends to be able to walk the beach, roam the woods, breathe fresh clean air, and experience the awe and splendor of sunrises and sunsets. As such, I try to be more conscious of doing my share to preserve our environment.

Sometimes I find myself laughingly counting how many more new cars I'll probably need to buy—then I pull myself back to the NOW moment, because it's all anyone really has, anyway! I remember getting perturbed with my mother when she would say: "Well, this is probably the last winter coat I'll buy." I used to tell her not to limit her life span with that kind of thinking. Now, sometimes, I have to remind myself not to repeat the same offense.

My values have shifted, and my priorities have changed. Remembering a friend's birthday with a letter suddenly becomes more important than marking off another task on my "to-do" list. I have vowed that I always want to be active, involved, and creative—but in a slower, more thoughtful and meaningful way. I want to enjoy the process and the beauty involved in the doing, rather than finding enjoyment in the completion so I can rush to do the next task. I truly look forward to embracing the last stage of life and bringing to it all of the accumulated wisdom and experience of earlier phases. Age does have its bonuses!

❖ SUMMING UP ❖

As we age, we need to take charge of our lives. The sooner we explore our options and make decisions that we can feel "right" about, the happier and more secure our future will be. Getting older in our society is a challenge, but one that can be met with dignity, grace, pride, and power if we have the will to look at the positive aspects of aging and make the decision to embrace them. Yes, we must look realistically at all aspects of our lives and make wise choices accordingly, and these choices can mean making our later years a time of continued growth, creativity, giving, and joy!

Action Steps

◆ Take care of emotional "unfinished business." This can be accomplished in a life review wherein we ask ourselves such questions as:

    a. To whom do I need to say "I love you"?

    b. What are some of my past mistakes, and what have I learned from them?

    c. What do I need to be doing with my life right now?

◆ Invite your closest friends to lunch or dinner to discuss your common issues with respect to aging as a woman alone.

    a. Make a list of alternatives that might work for each of the women.

    b. Honestly explore how you can support one another and to what degree you might be willing to do so.

    c. Consider meeting at least once a week for further exploration. You might want to use this book as a starting point. If the initial group doesn't share your enthusiasm, seek out other women who do.

◆ Take the necessary steps to facilitate and maintain your good health, as discussed in Chapter Five.

◆ Make sure you are "engaged" in life! Volunteer, travel, absorb yourself in a hobby, continue working if it feeds your soul—do what excites you!

◆ Check your local senior center, YWCA, and women's center for a listing of activities, as well as opportunities to serve. Get involved in your community!

◆ Repeat this affirmation each morning: *"I love life and embrace my eldership with joy as I learn new skills, open to new insights, and set new goals. I continue to find ways to be creative and productive, and I embrace the wisdom I've gained during my lifetime!"*

❖ ❖ ❖

CHAPTER EIGHT

POWER THROUGH PSYCHOSPIRITUAL GROWTH

*"Humans are close cousins of the snowflake in that
we too are infinite variations upon a starred pattern.
I urge you to discover your own variations."*

— *Jean Houston, author*

Psychologists, the clergy, writers, and many others who endeavor to help themselves and others live more fully have come to realize that it is impossible to separate our psychological selves from our spiritual selves. Growth in one area fosters progress in the other. Unfortunately, we often cheat ourselves by turning off in one area or the other because we have been wounded by a particular person or philosophy.

There are many schools of religious thought, each having unique views about the purpose of humankind and the nature of God. However, there is a distinction between the terms *religious* and *spiritual*. We all have a spiritual nature whether we are tuned into it or not; it is that part of us that is more than the body and the mind, that part that is our God connection, our Higher Power. Religion in its various forms, doctrines, and denominations is how humankind has put beliefs about God/spirituality into systems of thought and action. It is possible to be very spiritual, but not religious, just as it is possible to be religious, but not spiritual. Thus, when we talk about spiritual growth, we are talking about expanding our awareness of our Higher Power and inviting that transformative energy into our lives to bring about positive change, no matter what our particular religious orientation (or lack of it) may be.

There are many schools of psychological thought, each purporting to best define the human condition and its correlating emotions, each espousing views on how to most effectively help one's fellow man or woman. Most agree that the quality of our lives is connected to our beliefs and attitudes—that is, our "psychological state." We have found that progress is made by mounting the courage to look at ourselves honestly, by exploring and using the teachings we find helpful, and by allowing our spiritual and emotional natures to consciously blend and work together. When that happens, we experience a greater measure of peace and joy.

Journey Toward Wholeness

Our culture teaches women that the way to resolve any sense of incompleteness or emptiness in our lives is to find the right partner, and that any partner is preferable to being alone. This belief sets many of us off on a quest for the person that will fix it for us, and unfortunately, we all too often choose inappropriate, unresponsive, or abusive partners. Our underlying feelings of inadequacy or worthlessness may stem from a variety of sources, such as emotional or physical abuse and neglect as a child, alcoholic family members, or other traumas unrelated to the family of origin. Because the world is far from a perfect place, it provides myriad opportunities for us to deal with adversity from a very young age. If we allow the wounds from our childhood and adolescent battles to remain unhealed, the prognosis for developing a healthy relationship and/or a peaceful life is poor.

For years, Julie was stuck in misery and unproductive relationships. Gradually, "by the grace of God," she began to find the tools that helped her. She came to the realization that as long as her wounds remained raw and unbandaged, as long as she refused to examine them because she was afraid of dredging up pain, she would just keep repeating the same mistakes. Thus, she began to explore options that would help heal her—in both psychological and spiritual areas. As she took more responsibility for her own life instead of desperately searching for someone outside herself to "fix it" for her, she found the help and the answers that she needed in order to progress.

To the degree that a woman ignores her past, she is doomed to make unconscious choices in the present. It is vitally important to deal with our past, heal it, put it in perspective, see what can be gleaned from it, and acknowledge the many ways in which it impacts our thought processes in the present. It is critical for us to make peace with our parents and to make peace with ourselves, to forgive others and ourselves, to come to a point of understanding and compassion.

From this healthier place within ourselves, we can begin to gain some insight as to what our life purpose and our life path may be. At what age we begin to grow psychologically and spiritually is not the most important issue; that we DO begin right where we are and move forward is what matters. We were both in our thirties when we crossed the boundary into a more serious and systematic pursuit of those goals, and we have discovered that it is never too late to heal a trauma or learn from a situation, no matter how long ago it occurred. It is never too late to find new meaning and purpose in life, never too late to step out of a victim mode, never too late to discover our own unique beauty and spiritual power.

Balancing the Inner Male and Female

We all have masculine and feminine energy within us, and it is important for us to claim both energies and to balance them. If a woman is desperately searching outside herself for a man to complete her, she is doomed to failure. WE are the only ones who can complete us. The perfect marriage is the inner marriage, the balance and blend of our masculine and feminine energies.

Our society fosters an imbalance by creating a chasm between the sexes. It teaches us that the only way to fulfillment is to have an opposite-sex partner to express the energy we aren't allowed to own and express for ourselves. For example, a man who cannot allow himself to cry often chooses a sensitive woman to express the more sensitive side of his nature. A woman who will not allow herself to be assertive often chooses an aggressive man to express that particular side of her nature. This arrangement comprises two incomplete personalities striving to form a whole one by joining forces. However, it doesn't work that way. When two halves merge, the result is usually a conflicted and unsatisfying relationship. In the words of bestselling author, Dr. Wayne Dyer, "In any relationship in which two people become one, the end result is two half people."

However, when we claim and heal both our masculine and feminine sides, when we balance and integrate them and get them working together in harmony and cooperation, we have a viable inner marriage. We feel more complete and at peace within ourselves. We release any desperate desire to find someone "out there" to fix us or complete us. It is just at this point that we are more apt to attract appropriate, supportive, and balanced significant others into our lives. Nevertheless, it's important to remember that when we are emotionally and spiritually at peace, we will be more comfortable and more at peace with ourselves, whether coupled or alone.

Solitude's Blessings

If we want to progress rapidly in our psychospiritual growth, we need to appreciate the blessings of solitude. Solitude does not mean being alone and melancholy, wishing we were in the company of others. Solitude is a time of restful, creative, refreshing aloneness that expands and empowers us. People in our modern society are all too often frantically busy, and we accept the notion that our lives are somehow more fulfilled if we are constantly on the go. Many people become bored, restless, and lonely on Sunday afternoons because they are not at peace with themselves. Keeping as busy as possible and creating a life that is overflowing with people and activities can become a habit that is difficult to break. The result is stress, burnout, and a feeling of emptiness.

When a woman finds a way to balance her life, to be maximally involved in the world while maintaining that deep connection with herself through periods of solitude, she gives herself a great gift. But just how much solitude is necessary? There is no set amount of time that is right for everyone. Some will require more alone time than others, and individuals will need different amounts at different times depending on what is transpiring in their lives. Temperaments vary, as do circumstances. For example, a single mom raising children will have to struggle to find that alone time. A woman who lives alone or has a room of her own where she can meditate by herself will find solitude easier to achieve, but perhaps more difficult to embrace.

When Julie lived by herself and felt that she had too much alone time, she experienced a mixture of emotions. At times, she appreciated the solitude and used her alone time to her best advantage; other times she just felt plain lonely. She discovered that one way to more effectively accept the advantages of her solitary state was to plan the time alone with specific activities, such as journaling or reading an inspirational book.

While attending college and mothering two children, Julie wasn't able to find enough time for solitude. Occasionally, she would just "pull the plug" and take a day away from classes to enjoy some quiet time when the children were in school. On one of those days she wrote the following poem:

I NEED A DAY

I need a day midst life's confusion
To stay alone, to be in the quiet.
I need a way to order confusion,
To foster illusion,
To dabble in paint, or write a poem.
I need a day to think thoughts freely,
Responding only to an inner demand.
I need a day of solitude so that
I may experience my Self,
Again—in command.

Solitude is an essential ingredient of creativity. We need time alone to think, to plan, to see how things might be put together in new combinations. The creative spark within each of us can only be ignited when we are not continually bombarded by the pressures of our chaotic world. Whether the goal is to paint a picture, write, compose music, or just to explore creative solutions to everyday life, we need uninterrupted time alone.

Solitude allows insights, healing, peace, and perspective to flow out into our daily lives. We can attain the wisdom to see the mundane and broken parts of our lives as the material our souls have chosen to work with; we can appreciate the fact that our wounds are opportunities for growth, opportunities to forgive and release, opportunities to transform ourselves into the loving and powerful beings we truly are. All this begins with the understanding that solitude is not a punishment. It is not a curse upon the lonely. It is a precious gift that can lift us up to new heights, if we will only honor and embrace it.

Learning Through the Mirror of Relationships

If we are women participating in community or other alternative living styles, if we live alone because we haven't found a satisfactory substitute, or if we have decided we truly enjoy living a solitary life, we will still find ourselves relating to other people, at least to some degree. We inevitably relate to the people with whom we work and play, to children or other family members who are part of our lives, as well as to a variety of other individuals everywhere we go.

It is possible to utilize these interactions as a means of self-discovery if we are committed to a path of psychospiritual growth and if we are willing to look honestly at ourselves. This process is an enlightening and enjoyable experience that can help us get more fully acquainted with ourselves and help us comprehend "what makes us tick."

When we speak of the mirror of relationships, we are talking about how other people often reflect the various parts of ourselves. Typically, we disown or are not consciously aware of these mirror images, and it takes some real gut-level honesty to be able to look at them objectively! It is usually easier if the qualities we see in others are admirable, but a little more difficult if the characteristics we see in others are not worthy of praise. Fritz Perls, the father of Gestalt Therapy, helped clarify this concept when he taught that all parts of a dream, even the most disturbing parts, represent significant parts of the dreamer. While there are other levels and types of dreams, usually we can gain much insight into our nighttime adventures by viewing characters and objects as symbolic parts of ourselves. It is also enlightening to realize that the way in which we respond to people in our everyday life tells us much about ourselves.

Ione found that her children were wonderful mirrors for her. When she would get upset at them for some reason, if she honestly looked at the trait that was bothering her, she had to admit that she also possessed those same qualities and/or faults herself. Since it was too disturbing to admit that she was not perfect, she could rage against imperfections in her sons instead. Once she began examining her own behavior, she was able to see the particular psychological trait she was exhibiting. She was projecting her irritation at herself outwardly onto her children. It was as if she thought that if she could change them, then she would automatically be redeemed herself.

In time, she came to the realization that other individuals in her life were also serving as effective mirrors for her, and that the old truism "liars hate liars, and cheats hate cheats" made sense in an entirely new way. She started to apply her own attitudes toward others' behavior to an understanding of the various aspects of herself. Her grasp of the dynamics of relationships and why some work better than others was enhanced immeasurably.

Even when women find themselves without a partner, they can still enjoy a rich assortment of relationships. Each relationship, whether in shared living or separate living spaces, holds within it the potential for growth if we are willing to utilize it. If a woman finds herself with others who are also interested in psychospiritual growth processes, it is a wonderful opportunity to consciously become collaborators on the pathway to awakening and to release all those inner processes that create separation between ourselves and our fellow human beings. We find that when we do let go of these aspects of our lives and psyches, we are also able to release that which serves to keep us separate from the spiritual or higher aspects of life.

We soon discover, as we understand the mirroring process and take responsibility for our own emotions and actions, that it is NEVER someone else that is the cause of any dissatisfaction we might feel in our lives; everything begins and ends with us. Nonetheless, we must learn to be kind to ourselves, to lovingly forgive ourselves for real or imagined transgressions. The more we understand and forgive ourselves, the more we will be able to extend that same grace to others. At the same time, the more we understand others, the more likely we are to understand ourselves. Working on ourselves needs to be a daily practice, and the present moment is always the best time to start on this path.

We, as women alone, can take advantage of this precious time in our lives when we are unattached to a particular partner and explore our own natures and become more adept at all kinds of interpersonal interactions. If we do so, we will be prepared for a fulfilling assortment of intimate (sexual or nonsexual) alliances with others. If our desire *is* to find a partner, how much better prepared we will be to choose wisely and to create a truly healthy, long-lasting relationship!

The Cosmic View

There is in all of us an organic process, a wisdom greater than our conscious mind, that selects the wisest course of action for our ultimate growth, a wisdom that has the potential for teaching the lessons we most need to learn. Each of us has a purpose for being in this lifetime, and that purpose is often greater than our conscious fears or desires.

How often have we wanted something, and then when we obtained it, it wasn't in our best interests to have it? The opportunity to learn to be wiser or a little more openminded definitely arises at those times. It pays to have faith in the Divine Order beyond our conscious control and beyond the limits of our finite minds.

Ione often reminds herself of these concepts as she reflects on her life. Her major desire at the age of 19 was to marry and have three or four children and live down on her Iowa farm forever! However, Life had different plans for her. First, after much difficulty, she gave birth to a wonderful son, but she was unable to have additional children. Moreover, the farming economy in the fifties and early sixties was plagued by drought and low prices, so trying to make ends meet was extraordinarily difficult.

The desire to have more children in her life and the need for financial security led her to return to college to get her degree in education and to become a teacher. After she started working and making a steady income, her husband was free to leave the farm and go back to college. They moved together to the Pacific Northwest and started on a whole new adventure. In this new environment, Ione was afforded many opportunities to learn and grow and become more proficient in her field. She had multitudes of children in her life, and she felt alive and enriched in a way that she had never known before. Eventually, she and her husband adopted a very troubled 9-year-old boy who became one of the joys of their lives. Now, at age 31, he is a computer whiz and a very solid and productive member of society.

Ione sometimes looks back and wonders where her adopted son would be now had her dreams of a large family and life on the farm manifested in the way she desired. She might still be on the farm, and she would have loved her child, but she would have missed this second son and all the joy he brings her. There are so many rich and varied experiences that she, along with her husband and natural son, would never have enjoyed back in the Midwest. When Ione returns to visit her family in Iowa, she always realizes that her life needed to progress exactly as it did. While there was certainly nothing innately wrong with her earlier desires, that path was not ultimately in her highest or best interests. She blesses the wisdom beyond her conscious mind that pushed her in another direction and led her down this more expansive pathway. Of course, it's only in retrospect that all this becomes so clear.

Ione is now more comfortable with being "in the flow." Even when she has to work through painful experiences and disappointments and has to release both people and expectations from her life, she is often able to enter into the excitement of "what's next!" Her faith that the Creative Energy of the universe is both loving and supportive, even when it appears otherwise at times, is the greatest security she has found. It is now all the reassurance that she feels she consistently needs.

A large number of women have found that embarking upon a psychospiritual journey becomes a primary transformational experience, a catalyst that helps them move out of the role of victim and empowers them to begin to take charge of their lives, often for the very first time. Although it certainly isn't a sudden and magical solution to all problems, most women on a serious path of growth can identify a specific time period when they felt a renewed sense of hope and could see things clearly—an epiphany, a moment of truth. This journey opens a wide vista of experiences and opportunities to those who have the will and the heart to choose a higher path.

It is interesting to note that both Gloria Steinem and Betty Friedan, early leaders in the feminist movement who fought so long and so hard for women's rights, both currently write quite freely of their inner journeys and the spiritual (not religious) components of their lives. Steinem's book, *The Inner Revolution,* and Friedan's book, *The Fountain of Age,* both offer insights into dimensions of life that lie outside the external physical world of work and materialism.

Certainly, those more practical issues are vitally important to our lives, but we will never truly progress on our respective paths until we incorporate psychospiritual healing into our thinking and actions. We move forward when we can acknowledge the dramas, the actions and reactions, and the early programming that requires our attention and healing; we markedly advance when we begin to grasp the larger spiritual laws that govern all of life.

Discovering New Directions

The intent of our Holo Center Community is to offer people love and encouragement while also providing them with an opportunity to discover and explore new psychological and spiritual dimensions within themselves. Most tell us that after their experiences here, their lives are never quite the same. We met one such woman several years ago when she joined one of our spiritual group sessions. Sandy was a nurse and had just left her physician husband because he was having an affair. She was shocked, confused, and obviously in pain. As she came together with other people who were seeking to find meaning in a world that is often lacking in that quality, she began to touch her inner core. She regularly attended the group and took her personal journey very seriously. She mastered meditation techniques and other processes that helped her move forward instead of staying stuck in bitterness and pain. She attended workshops and classes and read many inspirational and spiritual books. An enthusiastic, radiant woman today, Sandy recently purchased a parcel of land and intends to develop a community of her own with a focus on responsible ecology and psychospiritual growth. She has traveled extensively in recent years and has been able to find or help create a sense of community wherever she goes.

Cathy had also just begun her deeply personal journey when we first met her. She joined a meditation group that met weekly while

Ione and Masil were still building the Holo Center's physical structure. Cathy had been in an abusive relationship and was beginning to see herself as more than just a body to be bruised and battered. She was learning that she had a mind and a spirit that was asking to expand and grow. Because she allowed that expansion to take place, she has been led down a path of varied experiences that have opened her up to ever-widening degrees of healing and insight. Today, with her life much more stable and solid, she is single-parenting her child and working as a therapist to help others discover the joys of personal growth. Like all of us, she faces challenges, but she now has the resources to deal with them and to move forward.

Julie is another example of someone who walked from the mire of self-pity and desperation out into the light and fresh air of growth. A turning point came for her one day when one of her students presented her with a book critique about the infallible order of the universe and the possibility of reincarnation. Although she was skeptical about the ideas, she was intrigued. She purchased the book and read it. Afterwards, she remembers getting down on her knees and thanking God, as she knew God then, for allowing her to see that perhaps the universe did make sense after all! As a result, Julie took a meditation class and practiced daily; she read and studied spiritually oriented books, and eventually started to apply spiritual principles to her daily life. Eventually, she decided to become a minister and spiritual counselor. She has no doubt that her psychospiritual explorations saved her life.

Our life here at the Center is filled with people coming and going in and out of various phases of their journeys toward individuation and wholeness. It is our joy to embrace people in the midst of their growth and to see them expand and change over the weeks, months, or years. We have found a lifestyle that allows time for our progression on the personal psychospiritual path toward wholeness, while allowing us to participate in that great adventure with many others. Sometimes, we are the teachers and role models; at other times, we are the students. The ebb and flow of life, the giving and receiving of wisdom, the sharing of love and understanding, all make for a rich and overflowing existence—a reason for Being!

One young woman who came for a week's intensive experience of emotional healing work was moved to write a poem about her time at the Center and to present it to us as a gift:

SISTERS

Oh great sisters!
Nomads, Warriors and Saints,
I drink of your words like sweet wine,
intoxicated by the rich, electric taste of insight.
Your delicate wisdom beckons to me,
irresistible calls to truth,
like the broad-winged spirit-guided angel
that awaits my arrival upon an impending death.
Warmed and nourished,
I rejoice in your laughter
like swimming in coils of sunshine
that wrap gently around my soul.

Frightened but eager,
I tremble with my pain
like a courageous child
awkwardly dancing the beat of a given destiny.

Led by the duty of truth,
Spirit has touched me
Yours, Mine, The One.
Aroused and shaken

I move forward like a child chasing butterflies
in the meadow of the dawn.

Oh great sisters!
Thank you for your presence and warm embrace
The silent whisper of your soul tickles my heart,
awakening a long forgotten fire.
The message, I hear—
Raise the gates of joy and burn with crimson faith
for upon the wings of compassion,
salvation awaits.

— LeAnn Anderson

Transformational Exercises

The following meditations and activities can be performed while alone, with one other person, or with a group. If you are alone, it is helpful to record notes on each experience in your journal. You may want to tape some of the exercises so that you can remain relaxed with your eyes closed. If you are with another person or a group, you may wish to have one of the participants read the exercise and then share with each other what you've experienced.

These activities call for the use of active imagination, visualization, and an open and receptive mind and heart. It is important to know that people visualize in different ways. Some see pictures, such as those on a movie screen. Others just think the thought. When people read a descriptive passage in a book, each reader experiences it in a slightly different way, uses their imagination in a unique fashion. However you react to the following exercises, they will no doubt be of value to you if you approach them with a sincere desire to move forward on your psychospiritual path.

Nature Walk

(If in a group, agree not to speak to one another until the walk is over.) Walking outdoors is a healing and antidepressive activity. Walking with the intention of tuning into, honoring, and listening to our natural surroundings for a personal message can be a useful and uplifting experience. Native Americans have always known that this is so. The setting for your nature walk can be your own backyard, a park, churchgrounds, the beach, or a nature trail. Walk and observe your surroundings; be open and receptive. When you are attracted to something, get as close as you can to it. Express (silently with your thoughts and feelings) your appreciation for it, and then listen to what it has to tell you. Thank it for its message and move on, staying open to other objects and messages. Write down or draw your experiences and observations before you speak with anyone, and then share if appropriate.

Finding and Loving the Little Girl Within

No matter what our chronological age, we still have our child's energy within us, and that child affects our adult life, our adult decisions, our adult reactions. Finding and healing and honoring that inner child can be a lengthy process and is the subject of many books and workshops. The following exercise is an initial step, and we hope it will motivate you to do further work.

Sit in a comfortable chair and relax; take in a deep breath through your nose; hold it, and let it out through your mouth. Do this several times. Picture yourself surrounded by a protective white light and know that your Higher Power or God (or whatever name you choose) is with you. See or imagine a large meadow in springtime. Breathe in the fragrance of flowers, and feel a warm, gentle breeze on your face.

You discover a path and decide to follow it. You notice a large shade tree up ahead, and under that tree is a little girl waiting for you. Notice her age, her facial expression, what she's wearing. As you approach her, you realize that she has something to tell you or something to show you. Sit down next to her under the tree. Listen and observe, and answer any questions she has. (Reader: pause for two to three minutes.) Now, if the child is willing, take her hand and begin to walk through the meadow. It's okay to laugh and sing and play. (Pause—take the time to do this.) Now, open your arms and embrace the child; tell her you love her and that you will protect her and take care of her. Feel and see yourself and this precious child melting into each other, and both of you dissolving into the light. When you are ready, review your experience. Write it down and/or share it with whoever is with you.

Balancing Masculine and Feminine Energy

Masculine and feminine components live in each of us. Our masculine side is connected to our left brain and has thinking and reason and logic as its strengths. The feminine component is connected to our right brain and reflects emotion and intuitiveness and creativity. An inner marriage takes place as these opposites are blended and balanced. When this phenomenon occurs, we stop trying to complete ourselves by looking outside for another to complete us. Complete already, we are less apt to enter into addictive relationships. Having a healthy relationship with ourselves, we are more likely to enter into healthy relationships with others.

To begin: Sit in a comfortable position and relax. Take in a deep breath through your nose; hold it; release the breath out your mouth. Do this several times. See yourself surrounded, enfolded, and protected by a flowing and beautiful white light that symbolizes your

Higher Power. See yourself on a sunlit beach. A gentle breeze is blowing, caressing your face as you look out over the water. Gliding toward you on your left is a beautiful, serene, and poised woman, your ideal woman. She is wearing a flowing gown of your favorite color. As she smiles at you, you can see and feel the warm glow of love that flows from her heart and into your heart. You can sense her warm and open nature, and you can appreciate her intuitiveness. She possesses all the many womanly traits and characteristics that you admire. She embraces you, and the two of you melt together and become one.

Approaching on the right is a dynamic and handsome man, the most perfect male creature that you have ever imagined, your ideal man. He is dressed like a bridegroom and as he smiles at you, you can see and feel the glow of love that flows into your heart from his heart. He is strong and wise; his mind is clear and logical; he is an organizer and planner. He possesses all the powerful traits and characteristics that you want to incorporate into your life. He embraces you, and the two of you dissolve together and become one. Now, blended inside of you is the most perfect male and female you can imagine, and you are empowered to call upon their love and wisdom whenever you wish.

Releasing People and Events

To the degree that we hang on to resentments and refuse to forgive others or ourselves for mistakes of the past, we block our own good and say no to our own peace and happiness, binding ourselves to our own pain. Forgiveness is what releases us from emotional pain and what opens up our future to new possibilities. Since forgiveness is a process, something like peeling away the layers of an onion, the following exercise needs to be repeated as many times as it takes to achieve satisfaction.

> Sit in a comfortable position and relax. Take a deep breath through the nose, hold it, and release it slowly through the mouth. Do this several times. Know that you are surrounded and protected by white light, the symbol of your Higher Power. Bring to mind a person or situation you need to forgive (it may be yourself). Allow your emotions to surface—feel whatever you feel. Now, see a Being of Light standing beside you, loving and encouraging you. The negative energy between you and who or what you need to forgive creates bondage. (Love is a moving energy and never creates bondage.) See this bondage in physical form as ties that can appear as thick as ropes or as thin as spider webs. They are wrapped around you and entangled with the other person or situation. The Being of Light gives you a wand that is as powerful as a laser beam and instructs you to cut through the ties. Take the wand of light in your hands, and then take all the time you need to sever the bondages. If you have trouble, ask the Light Being to help you. See the ties drop away. Feel the lightness and freedom. Affirm: *I forgive; I release.* See the person or situation surrounded by light and moving toward their highest good. Feel love and light permeating your every cell, your every thought and feeling. Affirm: *I am free. I have forgiven. I move forward with a new enthusiasm for life. I am free.*

Burning Bowl Ceremony

This is another method that leads to forgiveness and release. It can be done privately or as part of a group. First, assemble the materials you'll need: a bowl or other receptacle that can contain the heat of burning paper, thin writing paper, a pencil or pen. You might want to play some soft, inspirational music in the background.

> Begin by making a list on a piece of paper of people, things, events that you want to forgive and release. Just a word or a short sentence is sufficient for each item. Be open and receptive to guidance from your Higher Power with respect to what you need to put on the list. Know that you are about to engage in a powerful symbolic act whereby you will release old energy surrounding these people and events. You are freeing yourself to move forward in a new way; you are making more room in your life for dynamic life-enhancing power. Now, twist the paper so that it will burn easily, light it, and drop it into the bowl. Affirm: *As I forgive and release, I free myself to move forward into my Highest Good.*

All of these transformational exercises create a cumulative effect that is very powerful, so the more you practice them, the better your results will be. (We can attest to this fact because we use these tools ourselves.) Our fervent wish is that you may be inspired by some of the alternatives we've laid before you. May you begin a dynamic new phase of your life, no matter what your age or circumstance. Explore your alternatives and create a richer, fuller life than you've ever experienced before!

❖ SUMMING UP ❖

The best way for women alone, and indeed, for all humanity, to progress on the journey called Life is to continually search for the answers to those ageless, profound questions that have been posed with respect to the meaning of life. Both psychology and the spiritual dimension help us explore and probe our own inner depths, and it can be an exhilarating experience to discover the different aspects of who and what we are. It is equally rewarding to further examine the multidimensional aspects of the entire universe. We need to bestow the gift of exploration upon ourselves. To connect with our inner core is to connect with our totality!

Action Steps

◆ Do at least one transformational exercise each week until you have tried all five.

◆ Start a journal by writing a brief review of your life.

    a. What events have occurred in your life that have taught you a lesson of some sort?

    b. Think about situations that you would handle differently if you could. How would you change the outcomes? Would you be more loving? More assertive? Maybe a combination of both?

    c. Do you need to forgive someone? Do you need to make amends to someone?

    d. Are you willing to forgive yourself for real or imagined transgressions? Write down several things you now forgive yourself for doing. How do you feel?

◆ Seek out and attend at least one workshop, class, or seminar dealing with psychological or spiritual growth. It has been said that "when the student is ready, the teacher appears."

Once we make the decision that we want to learn and progress in some area, a source for that knowledge will come into our lives. It may be an individual, a class, a book, a lecture, or perhaps one of the Twelve-Step programs—there are many paths that lead to our ultimate destination. If we're not dogmatic about the specific starting point, many doors will open, and various options will present themselves.

◆ Form or join a small group that meets on a regular basis to support one another in psychospiritual growth. If the group is composed solely of women, consider studying *The Feminine Face of God.* (See the Recommended Reading section in the Appendix.)

◆ Read at least a few pages each day from some inspirational source. (See the Recommended Reading section in the Appendix.)

◆ If you are not already meditating regularly, take a class or use a "how to" meditation book to get started. *How to Meditate,* by Lawrence LeShan, is a wonderful introductory text that offers a variety of techniques.

◆ Begin to record and pay attention to your dreams. For further information, find a dream workshop and/or read the books of dream experts such as Tony Crisp, Patricia Garfield, Gayle Delaney, Ann Faraday, or John Sanford. (We also have dream interpretation instruction tapes, a "how-to meditate" tape, along with other growth tapes in our Tools for Transformation cassette set—see the Appendix.)

◆ Affirm often: *"My consciousness is ever-expanding as I learn and grow and move closer to infinite love and wisdom. I am a free and unlimited expression of God Life!"*

❖ ❖ ❖

CHAPTER NINE

EXPANDING AWARENESS:
A COSMIC PERSPECTIVE

*"The soul can split the sky in two
and let the face of God shine through."*

— *Edna St. Vincent Millay*

In the earlier years of our country's history, basic survival was part of everyday life, and men and women coupled out of the need to sustain themselves. Most people had little time to pay attention to anything beyond providing for the essential needs of the moment. Few had the time or energy, let alone the will, to question whether life was a truly satisfying emotional, intellectual, and spiritual experience. Having food on their tables, clothes on their backs, and a roof over their heads was so time-consuming that little thought was given to anything else, and in those fleeting moments when it was, the less pressing concerns of personal satisfaction and contentment were usually just quietly ignored or endured.

However, during the last half of the 20th century, when our country and the general population was becoming more affluent, we as individuals became more psychologically aware of the lack of meaning in our lives. Young people of the sixties started to question their family's lifestyle, wondering what it all meant. Many decried war and sought, often unsuccessfully, an elusive peace; they yearned for a world where love and brotherhood was the norm. Women rebelled against the inequalities in the workplace, in politics, and in their own homes, and started to demand more say as individuals and as a gender group. They started consciousness-raising groups to attune women to the injustices they had unconsciously lived with for so long. Sensitivity sessions, in various forms, sprang up on college campuses and in places such as Esalen, Asilomar, Berkeley, and other locations across the nation.

A new spiritual thirst developed as people sought a meaningful connection with something greater than themselves. Often this quest resulted in the adoption of different religious beliefs, with the charismatic movement gaining an unprecedented number of seekers. For many, the fundamentalist movement encompassed too much fear and restriction, so they sought expanded awareness through what was being termed the New Thought and the New Age movements. (It's interesting to note that the number of women in attendance at their events usually outstripped the number of men.) A deep hunger was growing in the hearts of many Americans, and women seemed to be most anxious for things to change. People were searching for new answers and new ways of living.

During the final decades of the 20th century, we have become aware of the need for healing the inner child, cognizant of the body/mind/spirit connection in issues of health, and have come to a greater understanding of the wide range of physical addictions, as well as the co-dependency of some relationships. We have begun to acknowledge the impracticality and ill-advisedness of what had long been accepted as "the way it is." We have deemed change necessary. Perhaps, it is for these reasons that increasing numbers of women are finding themselves alone.

Emerging Change

"When patterns are broken, new worlds can emerge."
—Unknown

Meaningful change usually means that old models have served their purpose and outlived their usefulness and have given way to new and more appropriate modes. This transition often necessitates a "breaking down" before a "rebuilding" can begin. This does not mean an end to deep personal intimacy and committed relationships. It might mean, however, that we are being called upon to create a new paradigm. It means that two, and in the case of those living in community, MANY complete people will come together to be loving, caring, and supportive of one another. It means learning to offer the quality of sustenance and compassion that will honor autonomy and the direction of each individual soul. It means we must face our jealousies, our inner fears and insecurities, and be willing to work on healing ourselves whenever we find we arc living in fear instead of love. We need to constantly remind ourselves that if we arc afraid of losing someone or something, it is a sure sign that we have not fully discovered ourselves or the connection to our divine source.

Before this new paradigm can emerge, however, we women must confront our ultimate aloneness courageously. We must wrestle with our inner demons and come to terms with relinquishing our roles as victims because we have not found the "right and perfect partner." Perhaps, at this very point of aloneness, we are with the right and perfect partner—OURSELVES! We, along with this inner companion, have work to do!

Statistically, with many women waiting until they're older to marry, with divorce rates increasing significantly over the last few decades, and considering that a woman's longevity is greater than that of a man's, many more women will find themselves alone—at least for sporadic periods throughout their lifetimes. And while certain moralists among us cry out that these statistics are a sign of our moral decay or depravity, perhaps what they see as a deterioration is, in all actuality, a necessary step in the evolution of relationships for the future.

We are not only about to enter into a new century, but into a new millennium. What contributions can we make to the incipient stages of the next 1,000-year era? Perhaps, as women alone, we are being called to help pioneer a new set of beliefs.

We are no longer merely a survivalist society. We have now reached a stage in the evolution of our culture where we can take a new and greater interest in our soul growth. While many so-called primitive cultures have been able to combine survival with their spiritual journeys through living closely to, and in harmony with, the earth, we have, on the whole, not been very successful in doing that.

Where interpersonal relationships are concerned, we must also acknowledge that the "bonds of matrimony" have often translated into the "bondage of marriage." Is it possible that the soul, in its evolutionary journey, is leading us in a new direction? The breaking down of traditional roles in our relationships may well signal a pivotal point in the formation of our future partnerships.

As women are given, and often forced into, more time alone, we must also come into a greater reliance of self. We have the opportunity for growth in new and untried directions. We are coming to the realization that we possess skills and talents far beyond what we've previously been cognizant of. We can revel in the new freedom we have to follow the course of our souls since we may no longer need to suppress our own inner urgings to care for spouses or offspring. Aloneness frequently becomes the opportunity for awakening, for determining new courses of action, for finding new paths to explore, and for offering gifts to the world. For, when we fully know ourselves and our own capabilities, we have more to give to others, whether it is to the universe at large, to a community, or to a significant other.

James Redfield points out in the Eighth Insight of his bestselling book, *The Celestine Prophecy,* that we need to grow beyond the co-dependent programming of our culture. We lose our opportunity for soul growth if we continue to play the traditional "needy" roles.

The philosopher Kahlil Gibran has written on marriage, "And stand together yet not too near together; For the pillars of the temple stand apart, And the oak tree and cypress grow not in each other's shadow." Gibran seemed to grasp our tendency to be co-dependent long before the term existed and before awareness of its unhealthy nature surfaced.

It is time to let go of the romantic notion that love means staring longingly into another's eyes while depending on that person to make us happy. In all honesty, this type of love seldom lasts "till death do us part," and many people spend much of their lives futilely chasing after the "happily ever after" illusion and end up being disappointed. Still others, for survival reasons, have stayed in unproductive relationships, forever feeling cheated. It never dawned on most of us that one of our tasks on this Earth is to complete ourselves! It is time for us to become strong, independent human beings capable of joining hands and forces, imbued with a willingness to take action to bring life on this planet closer to the perfection with which it was originally created.

Choosing to See Things Differently

Perception is everything! The time has come to modify our vision of what life "should be like" and to view the state of "being without a committed partner" within a larger context. If we can do so, we will begin to "see the big picture"—that is, appreciate the fact that the collective good can be of greater importance than our own individual experiences.

Life is neither senseless nor arbitrary no matter how much it may seem to be so at times. It always has a rhythm and purpose, and we must know that in the evolutionary and karmic scheme of things, there are reasons for every occurrence. Rocco Errico, the metaphysical Bible scholar, once said, "Life doesn't always seem fair, but it's accurate." So, as women alone, perhaps we are being called upon to be the pioneers of a revolutionary way of life, and we are being asked to play a significant role in this new model for life on our planet. Human nature seems to transform itself more expediently when we are being pushed into a corner than it does when we are in our comfortable ruts. Out of necessity, many women have not only created joyous and fulfilling lives for themselves, but in many instances, ones that they treasure even more than the traditional existences they may have left behind.

As we have visited with women across our country who have, for one reason or another, found themselves alone for short or even long periods of time, a few clear patterns have begun to emerge. Most women we've spoken to agree that in order for them to enter into another long-term, committed relationship, it must have more depth and purpose than the superficial partnerships they may have had in the past. Many women are enjoying their freedom so much that they would hesitate to partner again permanently. Others, while still desiring traditional relationships, admit that such a union would have to allow for large amounts of trust and autonomy and would need to be based on honest communication and a shared commitment to psychospiritual growth—factors that they did not necessarily consider in the past.

A significant number of women who have created community and/or extended families so love the diversity of their lives that they say it would be hard to confine themselves to living with one person. As the millennium approaches, what once functioned as the only preferred model for living is gradually becoming just one of many viable alternatives open to women (and men)!

This shift in perception asks much of women alone. But new paradigms always require courage, risk, and sometimes, extraordinary sacrifices and transformation among its creators—whether those involved are willing participants or not. We have found that many powerful women have been spurred on by a degree of fear, but they have persisted in their dreams in spite of their trepidation. Naturally, some efforts will be successful and some will not, but from each experience there is something to be learned, and the insights that are accumulated provide a foundation for the next endeavor.

Those of us who are older and more experienced, and who have garnered a little store of wisdom and financial security, can help other women of all ages and walks of life. We can be mentors for those who are not yet comfortable in their aloneness. We can share homes and resources of all kinds to foster another's independence. We can help empower our sisters by assisting them with low-interest loans, college scholarships, lodging at minimal cost, and so on, where and when that is possible. We can band together as soul sisters and make our experience of aloneness not just an issue or problem to be resolved, but an adventure that we can be excited and enriched by.

This can be a truly innovative and extraordinary time in our personal and collective histories. However, as women alone, we must be willing to see the cosmic overview and understand that the divine process is unfalteringly accurate. It has cast us in this position—not randomly, but with reason and purpose—because our soul knows this to be a necessary step in its evolution toward self-realization. It becomes clear that the old models of dependency must give way to wholeness and independence as we move closer to manifesting the divine perfection already within each one of us. Are you ready to join us in creating a new model that will allow for interpersonal relationships that are more loving and profound than they've ever been before? If so, let's join hands, look towards the future with a shared vision, and step into the 21st century with unrestrained enthusiasm!

❖ ❖ ❖

A P P E N D I X

RECOMMENDED READING

Ageless Body, Timeless Mind, Deepak Chopra. New York: Harmony Books, 1993.

As Someone Dies—A Handbook for the Living, Elizabeth A. Johnson. Carson, CA: Hay House, 1985.

Between Parent and Child, Hiam Ginott. New York: Avon, 1969.

The Boys and Girls Book about Divorce, Richard Gardner. New York: Bantam, 1985.

Cohousing: A Contemporary Approach to Housing Ourselves, McCamont and Durrett. Berkeley, CA: Habitat Press, 1988.

Dance of the Selves: Uniting the Male and Female Within, Loretta Ferrier. New York: Simon and Schuster, 1992.

Do I Have to Give Up Me to Be Loved by My Kids? Margaret and Jordan Paul. Minneapolis: Compcare, 1987.

Do What You Love, the Money Will Follow, Marsha Sinetar. Mahwah, NJ: Paulist Press, 1989.

Elegant Choices, Healing Choices, Marsha Sinetar. Mahwah, NJ: Paulist Press, 1988.

Empowering Children from Within: Education and Parenting for the 21st Century, Ione Jenson. Hayden, ID: I&J Publishing, 1993. To order, send $15.95 (includes postage) to E. 955 Grand Tour Dr., Hayden, ID 83835.

Families Apart, Melinda Blau. New York: Putnam, 1994.

The Feminine Face of God, Ruth Anderson and Patricia Hopkins. New York: Bantam, 1992.

Fire in the Soul, Joan Borysenko, Ph.D. New York: Warner, 1993.

From Soap Opera to Symphony, Julie Keene. Hayden, ID: I&J Publishing, 1993. To order, send $15.95 (postpaid) to E. 955 Grand Tour Dr., Hayden, ID 83835.

The Fountain of Age, Betty Friedan. New York: Simon and Schuster, 1993.

Growing Old Disgracefully, The Hen Co-Op, Freedom, CA: The Crossing Press, 1994.

Having Our Say: The Delany Sisters' First 100 Years, Elizabeth and Sarah Delany, with Amy Hill Hearth. New York: Kodansha America, 1993.

Healing Your Aloneness, Erika J. Chopich and Margaret Paul. New York: HarperCollins, 1990.

The Heroic Path: One Woman's Journey from Cancer to Self-Healing, Angela Passidomo Trafford. Carson, CA: Hay House, 1994.

How Shall I Live? Richard Moss, M.D. Berkeley, CA: Celestial Arts, 1985.

How to Meditate, Lawrence LeShan. New York: Bantam, 1984.

How to Achieve Total Prosperity, Mark Victor Hansen. Carson, CA: Hay House, 1981.

Learning to Love Yourself, Sharon Wegscheider-Cruse. Deerfield Beach, FL: Health Communications, 1987.

Losing Your Pounds of Pain—Breaking the Link Between Abuse, Stress, and Overeating. Doreen Virtue, Ph.D. Carson, CA: Hay House, 1994.

Love, Medicine,and Miracles, Bernie Siegel, M.D. New York: Harper and Row, 1986.

Love Yourself, Heal Your Life Workbook, Louise L. Hay. Carson, CA: Hay House, 1990.

Meditations to Heal Your Life, Louise L. Hay. Carson, CA: Hay House, 1994.

Ordinary People As Monks and Mystics, Marsha Sinetar. Mahwah, NJ: Paulist Press, 1986.

Positive Solitude, Rae Andre. New York: Harper/Perennial, 1991.

The Power of the Mind to Heal, Joan Borysenko, Ph.D., and Miroslav Borysenko, Ph.D. Carson, CA: Hay House, 1994.

Revolution from Within, Gloria Steinem. Boston: Little, Brown, 1992.

Seat of the Soul, Gary Zukav. New York: Simon and Schuster, 1990.

Spiritual Economics, Eric Butterworth. Unity Village, MO: Unity Books, 1983.

Staying on the Path, Dr. Wayne W. Dyer. Carson, CA: Hay House, 1995.

Thoughts of Power and Love, Susan Jeffers, Ph.D. Carson, CA: Hay House, 1995.

Wealth Without Risk, Charles J. Givens. New York: Simon and Schuster, 1988.

You Can Heal Your Life, Louise L. Hay. Carson, CA: Hay House, 1984.

Your Companion to 12 Step Recovery, Robert Odom. Carson, CA: Hay House, 1994.

Your Money or Your Life, Joe Dominquez & Vicki Robin. New York: Penguin, 1992.

SELF-HELP RESOURCES

Association for Children for Enforcement of Support
2260 Upton Avenue
Toledo, OH 43606
For information packet, call:
(800) 537-7072

Bag Ladies of the World
3530 High Street
Eugene, OR 97405
Send $8 ppd. for an audiocassette telling
how to start a group.

Elderhostel Service Programs
To order a catalog, write to:
P.O. Box 175
Wakefield, MA 01880

Elderhostel Travel & Learning Programs
To order a catalog, write to:
75 Federal Street
Boston, MA 02110

Foster Grandparents
1100 Vermont Ave. NW, 6th Floor
Washington, DC 20052

Gray Panthers
2025 Pennsylvania Ave. NW, #821
Washington, DC 20006
(202) 466-3132

Great Old Broads for Wilderness
P.O. Box 520307
Salt Lake City, UT 84152

Holo Center
E. 955 Grand Tour Dr.
Hayden, ID 83835
For a brochure or further information, send a self-addressed
stamped envelope to the above address.

International Folk Dance Directory
$10 from The Society of Folk Dance Historians
2100 Rio Grande
Austin, TX 78705-5513

Poetry $5 from Gordon Yaswen
740 First St. Sebastopol, CA 95472

Commission on Voluntary Service and Action
For a catalog of volunteer opportunities, send $9.95 to:
P.O. Box 117
New York, NY 10009
(800) 356-9315

Loners on Wheels
P.O. Box 1355
Poplar Bluff, MO 63901

National Association for Home Sitting Seniors:
David Sutherland
2119 E. Floyd Place
Englewood, CO 80110
(303) 761-1878

National Shared Housing Resource Center
431 Pine St.
Burlington, VT 05401
(802) 862-2727

Peace Corps
1990 K Street NW
Washington, DC 20526

Seniornet (American Online is host service)
399 Arguello Blvd.
San Francisco, CA 94118
(415) 750-5030

Tools for Transformation
Julie Keene and Ione Jenson
Audiocassette—8-tape set: $49 ppd.
E. 955 Grand Tour Dr.
Hayden, ID 83835

New Road Map Foundation
For the audiocassette album:
Transforming Your Relationship
with Money and Achieving
Financial Independence,
by Joe Dominquez, send
$60 ppd. to:
P.O. Box 15891
Seattle, WA 98115

Vista
1100 Vermont Ave. NW
Washington, DC 20525

Winslow Cohousing Group
For information, send $3 to:
353 Wallace Way NE
Bainbridge Island, WA 98110-1800

MORE SELF-HELP RESOURCES

The following list of resources can be used for more information about recovery options for addictions, health issues, or problems related to dysfunctional families. The addresses and telephone numbers listed are for the national headquarters; look in your local yellow pages under "Community Services" for resources closer to your area.

In addition to the following groups, other self-help organizations may be available in your area to assist your healing and recovery for a particular life crisis not listed here. Consult your telephone directory, call a counseling center or help line near you, or write or call:

American Self-Help Clearinghouse
St. Clares-Riverside Medical Center
Denville, NJ 07834
(201) 625-7101
(8:30 a.m. - 5:00 p.m. Eastern Time)

National Self-Help Clearinghouse
25 West 43rd Street, Room 620
New York, NY 10036
(212) 642-2944

❖ ❖ ❖

AIDS

AIDS Hotline
(800) 342-2437

Children with AIDS
Project of America
4020 N. 20th Street, Ste. 101
Phoenix, AZ 85016
(602) 265-4859
Hotline (602) 843-8654

National AIDS Network
(800) 342-2437

Project Inform
19655 Market Street, Ste. 220
San Francisco, CA 94103
(415) 558-8669

Spanish AIDS Hotline
(800) 344-7432

TDD (Hearing Impaired) AIDS Hotline
(800) 243-7889

The Names Project - AIDS Quilt
(800) 872-6263

❖ ❖ ❖

ALCOHOL ABUSE

Al-Anon Family Headquarters
200 Park Avenue South
New York, NY 10003
(212) 302-7240

Alcoholics Anonymous (AA)
General Service Office
475 Riverside Drive
New York, NY 10115
(212) 870-3400

Children of Alcoholics Foundation
P.O. Box 4185
Grand Central Station
New York, NY 10163-4185
(212) 754-0656
(800) 359-COAF

Meridian Council, Inc.
Administrative Offices
4 Elmcrest Terrace
Norwalk, CT 06850

National Association of Children of Alcoholics (NACOA)
11426 Rockville Pike, Ste. 100
Rockville, MD 20852
(301) 468-0985

National Clearinghouse for Alcohol and Drug Information
(NCADI)
P.O. Box 234
Rockville, MD 20852
(301) 468-2600

National Council on Alcoholism and Drug Dependency
(NCADD)
12 West 21st Street
New York, NY 10010
(212) 206-6770

❖ ❖ ❖

ANOREXIA/BULIMIA

American Anorexia/Bulimia Association, Inc.
418 East 76th Street
New York, NY 10021
(212) 891-8686

Bulimic/Anorexic Self-Help (BASH)
P.O. Box 39903
St. Louis, MO 63138
(800) 888-4680

Eating Disorder Organization
1925 East Dublin Granville Road
Columbus, OH 43229-3517
(614) 436-1112

❖ ❖ ❖

CANCER

National Cancer Institute
(800) 4-CANCER

Commonweal
P.O. Box 316
Bolinas, CA 94924
(415) 868-0971

ECAP (Exceptional Cancer Patients)
Bernie S. Siegel, M.D.
1302 Chapel Street
New Haven, CT 06511
(203) 865-8392

❖ ❖ ❖

CHILD MOLESTATION

Adult Molested As Children United (AMACU)
232 East Gish Road
San Jose, CA 95112
(800) 422-4453

National Committee for Prevention of Child Abuse
322 South Michigan Avenue, Ste. 1600
Chicago, IL 60604
(312) 663-3520

❖ ❖ ❖

CHILDREN'S AND TEENS' CRISIS INTERVENTION

Boy's Town Crisis Hotline
(800) 448-3000
Covenant House Hotline
(800) 999-9999

Kid Save
(800) 543-7283

National Runaway and Suicide Hotline
(800) 621-4000

❖ ❖ ❖

CO-DEPENDENCY

Co-Dependents Anonymous
P.O. Box 33577
Phoenix, AZ 85067-3577
(602) 277-7991

❖ ❖ ❖

DEBTS

Debtors Anonymous
General Service Office
P.O. Box 400
Grand Central Station
New York, NY 10163-0400
(212) 642-8220

❖ ❖ ❖

DIABETES

American Diabetes Association
(800) 232-3472

❖ ❖ ❖

DRUG ABUSE

Cocaine Anonymous
(800) 347-8998

National Cocaine-Abuse Hotline
(800) 262-2463
(800) COCAINE

National Institute of Drug Abuse (NIDA)
Parklawn Building
5600 Fishers Lane, Room 10A-39
Rockville, MD 20852
(301) 443-6245 (for information)
(800) 662-4357 (for help)

World Service Office (NA)
P.O. Box 9999
Van Nuys, CA 91409
(818) 780-3951

❖ ❖ ❖

EATING DISORDERS

Food Addiction Hotline
Florida Institute of Technology
FIT Hotline
Drug Addiction & Depression
(800) 872-0088

Overeaters Anonymous
National Office
383 Van Ness Avenue, Ste. 1601
Torrance, CA 90501
(310) 618-8835

❖ ❖ ❖

GAMBLING

Gamblers Anonymous
National Council on Compulsive Gambling
444 West 59th Street, Room 1521
New York, NY 10019
(212) 265-8600

❖ ❖ ❖

GRIEF

Grief Recovery Helpline
(800) 445-4808

Grief Recovery Institute
8306 Wilshire Blvd., Ste. 21A
Beverly Hills, CA 90211
(213) 650-1234

❖ ❖ ❖

HEALTH ISSUES

Alzheimer's Disease Information
(800) 621-0379

American Chronic Pain Association
P.O. Box 850
Rocklin, CA 95677
(916) 632-0922

American Foundation of Traditional Chinese Medicine
1280 Columbus Avenue, Ste. 302
San Francisco, CA 94133
(415) 776-0502

American Holistic Health Association
P.O. Box 17400
Anaheim, CA 92817
(714) 779-6152

The Fetzer Institute
9292 West KL Avenue
Kalamazoo, MI 49009
(616) 375-2000

Hospicelink
(800) 331-1620

Institute for Human Potential and Mind-Body Medicine
Deepak Chopra, M.D.
1110 Camino Del Mar, Ste. G
Del Mar, CA 92014
(619) 794-2425

Institute for Noetic Sciences
P.O. Box 909, Dept. M
Sausalito, CA 94966-0909
(800) 383-1394

National Health Information Center
P.O. Box 1133
Washington, DC 20013-1133
(800) 336-4797

The Mind-Body Medical Institute
185 Pilgrim Road
Boston, MA 02215
(617) 732-7000

World Research Foundation
15300 Ventura Blvd., Ste. 405
Sherman Oaks, CA 91403
(818) 907-5483

❖ ❖ ❖

IMPOTENCE

Impotency Institute of America
2020 Pennsylvania Avenue NW, Ste. 292
Washington, DC 20006
(800) 669-1603

❖ ❖ ❖

INCEST

Incest Survivors Resource Network International, Inc.
P.O. Box 7375
Las Cruces, NM 88006-7375
(505) 521-4260

❖ ❖ ❖

MISSING CHILDREN

National Center for Missing and Exploited Children
(800) 843-5678

RAPE

Austin Rape Crisis Center
1824 East Oltorf
Austin, TX 78741
(512) 440-7273

SEX ADDICTIONS

National Council on Sexual Addictions
P.O. Box 652
Azle, TX 76098-0652
(800) 321-2066

❖ ❖ ❖

SMOKING ABUSE

Nicotine Anonymous
2118 Greenwich Street
San Francisco, CA 94123
(415) 750-0328

❖ ❖ ❖

SPOUSAL ABUSE

National Coalition Against Domestic Violence
P.O. Box 34103
Washington, DC 20043-4103
(202) 638-6388 (800)
333-7233 (crisis line)

❖ ❖ ❖

STRESS REDUCTION

The Biofeedback & Psychophysiology Clinic
The Menninger Clinic
P.O. Box 829
Topeka, KS 66601-0829
(913) 273-7500

Rise Institute
P.O. Box 2733
Petaluma, CA 94973
(707) 765-2758

The Stress Reduction Clinic
Jon Kabat-Zinn, Ph.D.
University of Massachusetts Medical Center
55 Lake Avenue North
Worcester, MA 01655
(508) 856-1616

ABOUT THE AUTHORS

Ione Jenson is a counselor, dream therapist, and teacher who holds degrees in education, psychology, and counseling. She is the author of a self-published book, *Empowering the Child from Within: Education and Parenting for the Twenty-First Century,* has taught classes at the University of Oregon, and served as a special projects editor for Coronet Educational Films. For the past several years, Ione has been conducting workshops and doing private spiritual counseling. She is co-founder of the Holo Center, a retreat community in Hayden Lake, Idaho.

Julie Keene was formerly a professor at Ferris State University in Michigan, where she taught literature, composition, and a course in women's studies. She was a president of the women's faculty and a member of the faculty governing body. Julie left teaching after 11 years to attend Unity Ministerial School. She has served Unity churches in Columbia, Missouri; Coeur d'Alene, Idaho; and Tallahassee, Florida. She now works and lives at the Holo Center in Idaho and conducts workshops with a focus upon spiritual and psychological growth. She recently completed an autobiographical work called *From Soap Opera to Symphony.*

❖ ❖ ❖

We hope you enjoyed this Hay House book.
If you would like to receive a free catalog featuring additional
Hay House books and products, or if you would like
information about the Hay Foundation, please write to:

Hay House, Inc.
1154 E. Dominguez St.
P.O. Box 6204
Carson, CA 90749-6204

or call:

(800) 654-5126

❖ ❖ ❖